STUDIES IN ENGLISH LITERATURES

Edited by Koray Melikoğlu

Paola Brusasco

Writing Within/Without/About Sri Lanka

Discourses of Cartography, History and Translation in Selected Works by Michael Ondaatje and Carl Muller

STUDIES IN ENGLISH LITERATURES

Edited by Koray Melikoğlu

ISSN 1614-4651

6   *Wei H. Kao*
    The Formation of an Irish Literary Canon in the Mid-Twentieth Century
    ISBN 978-3-89821-545-9

7   *Bianca Del Villano*
    Ghostly Alterities
    Spectrality and Contemporary Literatures in English
    2nd, revised editon
    ISBN 978-3-89821-714-9

8   *Melanie Ann Hanson*
    Decapitation and Disgorgement
    The Female Body's Text in Early Modern English Drama and Poetry
    ISBN 978-3-89821-605-5

9   *Shafquat Towheed (ed.)*
    New Readings in the Literature of British India, c.1780-1947
    ISBN 978-3-89821-673-9

10 *Paola Baseotto*
    "Disdeining life, desiring leaue to die"
    Spenser and the Psychology of Despair
    ISBN 978-3-89821-567-1

11 *Annie Gagiano*
    Dealing with Evils
    Essays on Writing from Africa
    ISBN 978-3-89821-867-2

12 *Thomas F. Halloran*
    James Joyce: Developing Irish Identity
    A Study of the Development of Postcolonial Irish Identity in the Novels of James Joyce
    ISBN 978-3-89821-571-8

13 *Pablo Armellino*
    Ob-scene Spaces in Australian Narrative
    An Account of the Socio-topographic Construction of Space in Australian Literature
    ISBN 978-3-89821-873-3

14 *Lance Weldy*
    Seeking a Felicitous Space on the Frontier
    The Progression of the Modern American Woman in O. E. Rölvaag, Laura Ingalls Wilder, and Willa Cather
    ISBN 978-3-89821-535-0

15 *Rana Tekcan*
    The Biographer and the Subject
    A Study on Biographical Distance
    ISBN 978-3-89821-995-2

Paola Brusasco

WRITING WITHIN/WITHOUT/ABOUT SRI LANKA

Discourses of Cartography, History and Translation in Selected Works by Michael Ondaatje and Carl Muller

ibidem-Verlag
Stuttgart

Bibliografische Information der Deutschen Nationalbibliothek
Die Deutsche Nationalbibliothek verzeichnet diese Publikation in der
Deutschen Nationalbibliografie; detaillierte bibliografische Daten sind im
Internet über http://dnb.d-nb.de abrufbar.

Bibliographic information published by the Deutsche Nationalbibliothek
Die Deutsche Nationalbibliothek lists this publication in the Deutsche Nationalbibliografie;
detailed bibliographic data are available in the Internet at http://dnb.d-nb.de.

Cover illustration: Ceylon (Sri Lanka), conquered by the V.O.C. in the 17th century. Nicolaas Visscher. Source: http://commons.wikimedia.org/wiki/File:Insula_Ceilon_olim_Taprobana_Incolis_Tenarisin_et_Lankawn_%28Nicolaas_Visscher%29.jpg. Public domain.

∞

Gedruckt auf alterungsbeständigem, säurefreien Papier
Printed on acid-free paper

ISSN: 1614-4651

ISBN-13: 978-3-8382-0075-0

© *ibidem*-Verlag
Stuttgart 2010

Alle Rechte vorbehalten

Das Werk einschließlich aller seiner Teile ist urheberrechtlich geschützt. Jede Verwertung außerhalb der engen Grenzen des Urheberrechtsgesetzes ist ohne Zustimmung des Verlages unzulässig und strafbar. Dies gilt insbesondere für Vervielfältigungen, Übersetzungen, Mikroverfilmungen und elektronische Speicherformen sowie die Einspeicherung und Verarbeitung in elektronischen Systemen.

All rights reserved. No part of this publication may be reproduced, stored in or introduced into a retrieval system, or transmitted, in any form, or by any means (electronical, mechanical, photocopying, recording or otherwise) without the prior written permission of the publisher. Any person who does any unauthorized act in relation to this publication may be liable to criminal prosecution and civil claims for damages.

Printed in Germany

Contents

Acknowledgements	ix
Preface by Geetha Ganapathy-Doré	xi
Introduction	1
1 Cartography and Mapping	7
1.1 Western Images of Sri Lanka	21
2 The Making of History	41
2.1 History and the Construction of Identities in Sri Lanka	62
3 Language and Translation	77
3.1 Writing in English in Sri Lanka	98
4 Writing Within/Without/About Sri Lanka	107
4.1 Michael Ondaatje: Without (and About) Sri Lanka	107
4.1.1 *The English Patient:* A Eulogy of Deferral	109
4.1.1.1 "I didn't give them a right name."	109
4.1.1.2 "Cul-de-sacs within the sweep of history"	118
4.1.1.3 "Words, Caravaggio. They have a power"	122
4.1.2 *Running in the Family*: A Piecemeal Sketch of a Family, a Country, an Era through Journeys and Rumours	127
4.1.3 *Anil's Ghost*: The Ordeals of Identity	135
4.2 Carl Muller: Within and About Sri Lanka	152
4.2.1 *The Jam Fruit Tree, Yakada Yakā, Once Upon a Tender Time*: Bittersweet Scenes of a "madcap, merry lifestyle"	154
4.2.2 *Colombo: A Novel*: Deconstructing the City	172
Conclusions	185
Bibliography	187

Acknowledgements

I would like to thank the people that in different ways helped me during my research and while writing this piece of work.

While in Sri Lanka and after, precious suggestions for research came from Prof. Rajiva Wijesinha of Sabaragamuwa University, Prof. Siromi Fernando of the University of Colombo and Prof. Walter Perera of the University of Peradeniya, who also helped me realize my wish to meet Carl Muller and to participate in the ceremonies of the Graetian Prize 2005, while the English Department at the University of Colombo and the International Centre for Ethnic Studies were invaluable sources of archival material.

For opening their homes and minds to me, my special thanks go to Carl Muller for his entertaining and most interesting conversation and to Anne Ranasinghe who shared with me her views on writing and some of her memories and expatriate experiences in Sri Lanka.

Thought-provoking reflections also came from meeting at conferences in Italy Prof. Suresh Canagarajah and Prof. Charles Sarvan, who kept contributing their perspectives from abroad.

Thanks also to Professors Valerio Fissore, Carmen Concilio and Renato Oliva of the University of Turin for their comments and suggestions along the way, and to Professors Donatella Abbate Badin and Melita Cataldi for their encouragement at all times.

Affectionate thanks to my family, my friends and John for their warm support.

Paola Brusasco

Preface

Paola Brusasco's *Writing Within/Without/About Sri Lanka* is a bold attempt to resemanticize post-colonial studies by interweaving history and geography, theory and literature, language and culture in a densely conceptualized study focusing on the novels of Michael Ondaatje and Carl Muller, two authors of Burgher origin.

Though talented and highly acclaimed authors from Sri Lanka have put English Writing from Sri Lanka in the literary map of the world, it remains somewhat overshadowed by its more noisy and conspicuous neighbour, i.e., Indian Writing in English. This is partly due to the civil war in Sri Lanka that lasted for more than a quarter of a century and damaged the country, its people and its image. Anthologies like *Penguin New Writing from Sri Lanka* or *Kaleidoscope: An Anthology of Sri Lankan English Literature* (by D. C. R. A. Goonetilleke, 1992 and 2007 respectively) and critical investigations like *Writing Sri Lanka: Literature, Resistance & the Politics of Place* (Minoli Salgado, 2007) and *Island Paradise* (Melanie A. Murray, 2009) have tried to academically bolster the weight of Sri Lankan writing in English. However, a book devoted specifically to the works of individual authors was much needed. Paola Brusasco's brilliant exploration of the Western and modern construction of the images of Sri Lanka and how they are shaped and continually altered by the gaze of contemporary writers living within and outside is a welcome intervention in English studies in general and post-colonial studies in particular. Her rich encounters on the field adequately inform her scholarly endeavour in the third space of Italy.

Issues of identity, intra- and international politics are themes that interconnect Ondaatje, who has moved away from Sri Lanka, and Muller, who has chosen to stay there. Both are translated men and postmodern map makers, according to Paola Brusasco. If Ondaatje depicts the interstitiality of world history in *The English Patient* and the fragmentation of a family across continents in *Running in the*

Family, he gives a transnational and transgendered perspective on Sri Lankan history in *Anil's Ghost*. Paola Brusasco looks at how Muller records the vanished and hybrid subculture of the Burghers in his semi-autobiographical trilogy. However, it is her analysis of Muller's radical geography and economy of difference in his deconstruction of the capital city of Colombo in his eponymous novel that stands out as very original and successful. The conclusion leaves us wanting for more, but the author has discreetly strewn names of other Sri Lankan authors in the text as signposts for a new exploratory journey to come.

Geetha Ganapathy-Doré
Associate Professor of English
Faculty of Law, Political and Social Sciences, University of Paris 13

Introduction

The choice to investigate Sri Lankan literature in English finds its justification in both the international reputation gained by a relevant number of its authors (Michael Ondaatje, Romesh Gunesekera, Shyam Selvadurai, Yasmine Gooneratne among others) and the awareness that the quality and the maturity reached by those writers who use English as their expressive medium in the former colony has been growing steadily and widening its scope, moving, as D.C.R.A. Goonetilleke (2005) points out, from the nostalgic rural atmospheres which characterized the first novels to a variety of themes that explore today's complex and layered reality.

Writing Within/Without/About Sri Lanka originates from a desire to analyze the ways in which Sri Lankan authors Michael Ondaatje and Carl Muller, who come from a similar background but have different personal histories, confront the issue of identity and its construction through discourses that span across cartography, history and language.

Both Ondaatje and Muller are Burghers, that is, members of a minority group that strictly speaking is formed by "the descendants of male European settlers under the Dutch East India company" (Mendis 1998, 64) but, in its broadest sense, has come to include people of variously mixed European and local ancestry, who have often been looked down upon as the degenerate offspring of the invaders. Both have English as their mother tongue, both have a deep preoccupation with history/ies, and both live a personal condition that suggests "translation" as a possible label for the heritage and experiences that have shaped their identities. What constitutes a major difference, though, is their relationship to Sri Lanka: while Ondaatje left the island in his pre-teens to reach his mother in England and from there moved to Canada, where he lives today, Muller has remained in his native country (except for a few years in the Middle East), coming to terms with the difficulties of being perceived as an outsider when nationalism was rampant, living through political and social changes that made his relation to Sri Lanka one of estrangement and belonging at the same time.

The language in which they write constitutes a marked trait in a country where English, the official language in the 150 years of British domination, was relegated to a secondary position after independence (1948) and then phased out in education and other fields of public interaction after the Official Language Act of 1956 decreed that Sinhala was to be the only tongue for education, administration and civil life in general. Muller occupies a particular position as, living in a country where the large majority of the population speaks Sinhala and over 20% speak Tamil, fluency in these languages is needed in order to have access to everyday life. Writing in English, then, is perfectly natural for him, but it is inevitably perceived as the expression of a marked and controversial identity that further reinforces the boundaries separating ethnic groups. Ondaatje, coming from a mixed Burgher-Tamil background in which, however, English was dominant, identified more and more with the language after completing his studies in England and Canada, so that today both his location outside his native country and the use of English distinguish him from his fellow countrymen/women.

In the ongoing process of redefinition of itself that started with independence in 1948, Sri Lanka has been facing serious problems which, as in many other countries formerly subjected to colonialism, largely derive from internal divisions mainly based on ethnicity, often exacerbated in the years of European domination by the policy of *divide et impera* implemented to maintain control. Thus identity – the definition of the self through an interplay of affiliation to and exclusion from social formations – is among the very fundamental issues that affect life in the country, to such a degree that outbursts of extreme violence and the meting out of supposed justice have been part of its continuing internal struggles. Ever since independence, in fact, relations between Sinhalese and Tamils started to deteriorate, with the result that for decades the country was trapped in a war that mainly opposed the Liberation Tigers of Tamil Eelam fighting for a separate state in the north to the government's refusal to yield sovereignty. The conflict deeply scarred the country when it peaked in 1983 and again in the late 80s and early 90s and, despite repeated attempts at conciliation involving also the international community, it was only in May 2009 that a harsh offensive by the army killed the Tigers' leaders and forced the fighters to admit defeat. Under these circumstances, then, ethnicity is the first parameter against which identity is measured in Sri Lanka, but the issue is further complicated by religion, social class or caste, language and provenance, so that it would be more appropriate to speak of layered, cross-cultural identities. Identity, and the social and cultural constructs that contribute to its shaping, are crucial for Ondaatje and Muller, for whom the cross-cultural aspects also include dealing with alienation, international and intranational cultures. To them, Rushdie's words apply perfectly:

> Our identity is at once plural and partial. Sometimes we feel that we straddle two cultures; at other times, that we fall between two stools. But however ambitious and shifting the ground may be, it is not an infertile territory for a writer to occupy. (1991, 15)

This piece of research has been written as an open investigation which combines the fundamental study of theoretical works of post-colonialism with an empirical journey in search of images, devices, motifs and instances of social criticism that in the texts analyzed engage with the issues mentioned above. Besides being recurrent sites of post-colonial studies, cartography, history and the relation to language constitute sensitive and significant areas of interest for Ondaatje and Muller, who have transposed in literary terms experiences of relocation and alienation in their own country which are inevitably intertwined with the "microhistory" each of us lives, and the "macrohistory" that shapes individuals, societies and countries.

While the themes highlighted are a kind of common ground for both authors, the focus of engagement varies. Thus, some theoretical assumptions at the basis of cartography and exploration find explicit treatment in Ondaatje's *The English Patient* (1992) and, to a lesser degree, in *Running in the Family* (1982), while Muller provides an example of literary topography in *Colombo – A Novel* (1995). History is probably the most fertile terrain for both: Ondaatje, who, quoting John Berger, wrote "Never again will a single story be told as though it were the only one",[1] interrogates constructions of ancient and contemporary history in *Anil's Ghost* (2000), while Muller, for whom the writer's primary task is that of "righting the nation",[2] provides in the so-called Burgher trilogy an ironical depiction of twentieth-century Sri Lankan history as lived by the Burghers, but keeps shifting from the time of the narration to the beginning of the colonial era retracing the arrival of the Portuguese, the Dutch and the British from the sixteenth century onward. Language as an identity marker and therefore as a key to a feeling of rootedness and belonging features in the three texts by Ondaatje mentioned so far, and takes additional representational value in Muller's trilogy, where it is manipulated to obtain comic portrayals of the various ethnic groups.

The main body of this study consists of four chapters: three devoted to theoretical issues and one which analyzes the texts chosen. The general frame of reference is derived from poststructuralism, deconstruction and post-colonial studies, but in keeping with the recent call for analysis to focus on specific situations and highlight their peculiarities instead of restating universalizing visions, each chapter presents a general discussion of the topic and closes with a section which restricts its scope to the specificity of Sri Lanka. Thus,

---

[1] The sentence appears on the frontispiece of *In the Skin of A Lion* (Toronto: McClelland and Stewart, 1987).
[2] From the title of an article published in *The Island*.

although the premises laid in the first three chapters sometimes overlap the domain of cultural studies and anthropology, it is a slant deemed necessary to substantiate and contextualize further analysis.

Chapter One reviews the most important Western principles and consequences of cartography, mapping and naming in the light of the mechanisms and conventions revealed by deconstruction and post-colonial studies. Geographical and linguistic studies have shown that maps are not objective representations but vary with the underlying ideology, while travel writing and journals, especially those dating back to the colonial era, often mirrored racial prejudice and orientalist expectations. The approach adopted follows Michel Foucault's theorizing on the construction of authority and reality through discourse, as well as Edward Said's and Elleke Boehmer's vision of the preparation, legitimization and maintenance of the British Empire largely as a textual exercise. The chapter closes with "Western Images of Sri Lanka", a sampling of a few passages from different epochs and genres meant to illustrate the constructions of the island through Western eyes.

Chapter Two is devoted to history and historiography, again interrogating the assumptions upon which they are founded. Referring especially to Foucault, Said, Antonio Gramsci, Homi Bhabha and Hayden White, history is looked at as a narrative, liable to be conditioned by subjectivity even when it is presented and perceived as an objective report based on facts. The constitutive elements of historical discourse are analyzed also with reference to the rhetorical strategies deployed in the production of history through journalism, and to the position of the Popular Memory Group based at the University of Birmingham, which strongly emphasizes the role of individual memory and voice. The concept of nation is then explored with particular attention to the ways in which its dangerous derivation, nationalism, thrives on historical constructs to promote exclusionary identities. The closing part of the chapter is a reading in this light of a few case-studies illustrating the creation of traditions and myths of origins in Sri Lanka meant to justify the territorial and political claims that fuelled the conflict for almost thirty years.

Even if the preoccupation with language and its use in ideologically connoted discourse underlies the whole research, it is Chapter Three that more explicitly investigates the linguistic strategies adopted in post-colonial writing and the similarities between the latter and translation that the recent "cultural turn" in translation studies has highlighted. Translation is looked at from multiple points of view: the cross-cultural movement of carrying something across conveyed by its etymology, the debate opened by post-structuralism and Jacques Derrida on representation and the notion of the original, Lawrence Venuti's advocacy of a foreignizing strategy to adequately render otherness. The culture-specific part of the chapter illustrates the language situation in Sri Lanka: its polyglossia, the social value of languages, the difficult relation between Sinhala and Tamil, as well as the current debate around the existence of a local variety of English and its literature.

Michael Ondaatje's T*he English Patient* (1992), *Running in the Family* (1982) and *Anil's Ghost* (2000), and Carl Muller's so-called Burgher trilogy, *The Jam Fruit Tree* (1993), *Yakada Yakā* (1994), *Once Upon a Tender Time* (1995), and *Colombo – A Novel* (1995) are analyzed in Chapter Four in order to see how cartography, history and language/translation are dealt with especially in relation to the question of identity. While attention is devoted to instances where the texts show subversive traits that undermine accepted "truths" or principles, my discussion also includes their rewriting of maps or alternative modes of representation, their emphasis on the versions of history, often silenced, that emerge from below or from memory, and the tension to which they submit the language in order to reveal its connivance with power and at the same time make it distinctly their own.

1 Cartography and Mapping

The Book of Genesis identifies the act of naming as that primal, divine action through which the world came into being. Between word and world, then, the Judeo-Christian tradition identifies a relationship that intrinsically acknowledges the power of the *logos* as the principle allowing creation. Following this line, a sort of absolute and intrinsic link seems to arise between name and object, and enormous power is ascribed to the action producing it as well as to its performer. Thus, signs and utterances bring reality into existence and, by extension, create the book of the world. And, because man too participated in the act of naming, the same power has often been attributed to him, so that starting from the so-called Age of Explorations, a growing confidence in human progress justified the vision according to which man was authorized to contribute his own inscriptions. This quasi-mystical perspective can be somewhat downsized by the consideration that, even embracing such a view, it is undeniable that man came second and whatever he gave name to was already there: nothing divine informed his action, no creation resulted. To bring secularism further, Ferdinand de Saussure's definition of language as a system of signs stressed the arbitrariness of the link between a word and the concept it calls to mind, while the positions of post-structuralists like Roland Barthes, Michel Foucault, Jacques Derrida and Jacques Lacan exposed the subjectivity and the strategies at work in every kind of discourse, and postulated the construction and embodiment of authority in virtually every text, an approach adopted by anthropologist James Clifford, who goes so far as to contend that any coherent presentation in itself "presupposes a controlling mode" (1988, 54).

Since naming – and in more general terms, language – plays a fundamental role in the construction of reality, post-colonial studies have built on post-structuralist analysis and deconstruction and shown how the creation of that peculiar reality known as the British Empire was facilitated through discourse operations. In fact, as E. Said has pointed out, empires came into existence as the product of the interaction of philosophical and imaginative processes related to the envisaging, acquisition and settlement of space. Therefore, military conquest and imposition were both anticipated and followed by legitimizing cultural constructs which promoted the consolidation of empire through what Elleke Boehmer (1995, 13) defines as "a textual exercise": consciously or not, political treaties, diaries, acts and edicts, administrative records, articles, letters, and especially journals and maps laid the foundations for European settlement and justified it in the eyes of those at home, while Western geographical and social models were implicitly accepted and portrayed in many canonical works of literature. Thus, geographical exploration and cartography played a major role in creating the assumptions for European colonialism and casting a scientific, progress-bearing light on the appropriation of the land.

Chris Tiffin and Alan Lawson maintain that "colonialism [...] is an operation of discourse, and as an operation of discourse it interpellates colonial subjects by incorporating them in a system of representation" (1994, 3). Reduced to signs, lands and peoples were thus inscribed within a wider text that allowed them to be read as functional to British domination. Language in this case was used to express – and impress – a fictional reality that met imperial requirements, while categorization through tropes like utopia, wilderness, the Garden of Eden, the noble savage, permitted to interpret the world in reassuring, self-repeating terms. The role played by travel writing and cartography in structuring such a system has been explored by many scholars (Tiffin and Lawson, Simon Ryan, Mary Louise Pratt, José Rabasa, Graham Huggan, to name but a few) who in the texts produced by explorers and cartographers see the basis for a convenient image of colonized countries. They contend that mapping is not a mimetic, innocent representation, but rather an activity deeply rooted in social constructs which produces a number of subtexts subliminally transmitted to mapreaders. This vision postulates the notion of space as a mental, physical and social product which cartographers keep re-writing and re-defining according to "an ever-shifting social geometry of power and signification" (Massey, quoted in Jacobs 1996, 5), a space that imperialism constructed according to supposedly universal terms of measurability and divisibility. Similarly, David Spurr argues that "the very process by which one culture subordinates another begins in the act of naming and leaving unnamed, of marking on an unknown territory the lines of division and uniformity, of boundary and continuity" (1993, 4). Thus, unopened and yet appealing territories and waters (which in English are tellingly defined "uncharted") were – intentionally or not – subjected to an effacing operation and represented as blanks, which in the eyes of Western readers *de facto* meant empty spaces. As gaps in knowledge became screens onto which European fantasies could be projected, indigenous populations, as well as any kind of division or mapping they might have adopted before the colonial encounter, were ignored, with the result that the land was perceived as uninhabited and open to exploration and conquest. Alternatively, matching the abundance of picturesque images of monsters, sirens, treasure chests and exotic or fabulous animals with which mythological cartography filled far-away spaces, on some maps native peoples were iconized as cannibals, which supported in the collective consciousness a compelling moral need for "civilized" nations to go and introduce them to humanity, on a Christian mission that very aptly conjugated the etymologically related notions of culture and colonization. The former approach was particularly true for Australia, where, as Ryan (1996) contends, emptiness compounded an age-long tradition of oddity and perverseness associated to it. Imaginative accounts of Australia described it as a place where nature assumed odd shapes, a place which, because of its antipodean position, functioned as the reverse of European civilization and values. Such a representation of Australia, still common in the seventeenth and eighteenth centuries to support the notion that a southern landmass was deemed necessary to counterbalance Europe and the countries in the northern hemisphere, also contributed to an all-out process of creating difference by recurring to opposition, that is, applying the logic of the binary system within the European process of othering the rest of the world.

In his study *Territorial Disputes,* Graham Huggan examines the authority of the map as an instrument of geopolitical claim. Beside "the combined effect of its diverse strategies: the delineation and demarcation of territory; the location and nomination of place; the inclusion and exclusion of detail within a preset framework; and the choice of scale, format, and design" (1994, 9), Huggan refers to J. B. Harley's uncovering of less evident techniques such as the omission of small but meaningful details, deliberate reorderings of visual signs which he terms "silences", "positional enhancements" and "representational hierarchies" aimed at suggesting social, cultural or religious layerings, and adjustments in projection so that the reader's attention is drawn to the region(s) where supremacy is to be found. In an interesting reflection, Susan Bassnett points out the similarities in the activity of the map-maker, the translator and the travel writer, who "are not innocent producers of text" (1993, 99), but rather enact a manipulative process that conditions the receiver's perception and attitude to the object depicted. Bassnett identifies a telling example in the map published in *The Independent* in 1992 portraying the new Europe resulting after the collapse of the communist regimes: as Eastern and Western Europe had come to mean political entities rather than geographical terms, the disappearance of the ideological layer of signification finally allowed the repositioning of Vienna more to the east than Prague.

In spite of their being based on personal experience and socio-cultural projections, travel writing and geographical maps have often been regarded as objective and mimetic representations of reality, thus ignoring the specific perspectives from which they issued. Inevitably, explorers perceived the landscape according to their cognitive abilities and cultural models, and the reproductions they gave involved a selection of the features to portray. Moreover, as Ryan points out, first sightings were usually anticipated by the creation of expectations regarding the goal, whereby the roughly imagined presence of unknown lands had already been filled with hypotheses and hopes about what their features might be, according to a frame of reference which inevitably pre-determined to a certain extent the perception of the explorer.

The Latin saying *veni, vidi, vici* synthesizes the imperial enterprise: the actions of arrival and conquest are bridged by the gaze, which becomes an instrument of "construction, order and arrangement" (Spurr 1993, 14) and together with aesthetic pleasure also provides elements of information and authority. Spurr relates this commanding view to Foucault's reflections on the panopticon, J. Bentham's circular prison, whose structure allowed control of every single cell from the vantage point of an unseen observer in a central tower. Although generally speaking the gaze can be bidirectional, in this model power is conferred only to the centre, with the other extremity of the line experiencing it as an inescapable constraint, while at the same time the accumulation of the gazes coming from a plurality of subjects sanctions the strength of the focal point. As in Lacanian psychoanalytical terms self-identity is constituted within the gaze of another, here it is the directionality of the unequal gaze that expresses power so that, Foucault suggests,[3] authority is to some degree conferred by those who obey it. Similarly, the point of view adopted in maps or travel writing is usually either outside and above the landscape portrayed or right at the centre, but in both cases it is a detached and authoritative position whose *raison d'être* lies in the visual activity which exploration consists of. Jacobus Coetzee, J. M. Coetzee's fictional explorer in *Dusklands* (1974), experiences both omnipotence over and identification with the scene observed:

---

[3] Michel Foucault, *Discipline and Punish: The Birth of the Prison*, trans. Alan Sheridan (New York: Pantheon Books, 1977).

> Nothing is hidden from the eyes. As the other senses grow numb or dumb my eyes flex and extend themselves. I become a spherical reflecting eye moving through the wilderness, and ingesting it. [...] I am all that I see. [...] What is there that is not me? (1974, 84)

He seems to be feeling the kind of anxiety that prompts travel writers to insist on declarations of truth and faithfulness while trying at the same time to deny self-identification with the environment in order to guarantee objectivity. The fact that such inevitable "inherent relativity" (Ryan 1996, 101) has generally been ignored depends on the one hand on a widespread acceptance of a mode of representation the Western world was familiar with, and on the other hand on a heroic, mythological aura surrounding explorers, who in the collective imagination replaced the medieval hero on a long and perilous quest for ultimate knowledge and real self. Backed by the etymological relation that goes back to its French and Latin precursors – *travailler* and *trepalium* (an instrument of torture) – "travel" very aptly includes a number of meanings: "torment", "toil", "put to work", "gain knowledge through study", "suffer the pains of childbirth" (*New Shorter OED*), all of which merge in different degrees in the image of the adventurous explorer, whose enterprises were often celebrated as glorious progress in universal knowledge. A paradigmatic example of how discourse operations can tailor the coverage of events for propagandistic purposes is given by Tiffin and Lawson reporting newspaper headlines and official speeches in which news of Tensing and Hillary's ascent of the world's highest mountain, Chomolungma, on the eve of the coronation of Elizabeth II was saluted as Sir Hillary climbing Mt. Everest and adding "the brightest jewel of courage and endurance" to the Crown (1994, 1).

The manliness of exploring missions was compounded by the portrayal of the conquered landmass as feminine: "virgin", "untouched", "unveiled" territories whose "bosom", "charms", "depths" the explorer "penetrated", "cleaved", "pierced", "opened"; the abundance of metaphors basically generates two images of femininity: the alluring yet coy woman who opposes resistance but finally surrenders to a taming power, and the castrating female constantly threatening man with her engulfing mystery. In different ways, both call for male presence, but the danger embodied by the latter image posits the explorer as a voyeur who cautiously observes and describes from a distance. The frequent equation wilderness/ nothingness, moreover, supports the idea of the land as a female body waiting to be fertilized by man, or the land as potential bearer of a meaning to be generated by man. In his perusing the land-woman-text (in its fullest sense of "wear out by use, examine, travel through exploringly, read through"), the explorer/ cartographer enacts one of the instances of the link between eros and language that George Steiner sees as permeating human relationships: "Intercourse and discourse, copula and copulation, are sub-classes of the dominant fact of communication" (1975, 38) and, thinking of the choice of vocabulary that characterizes travel journals, one would be tempted to reverse Steiner's statement, "Sex is a profoundly semantic act" (1975, 38), into "semantics is a profoundly sexual act". The sexual overtones in Steiner's model of the translation process may arguably be detected in the explorer/cartographer's activity, itself an interpretation and translation of signs into another code: the first step, "initiative trust", or the expectation that the work will yield something, is followed by "appropriative penetration", an aggressive mode which in its definition refers to both economic acquisition and sexual domination. The text/land is then "naturalized", that is, incorporated into a familiar system, at which stage some kind of restitution can finally take place, so that a new balance is settled. The analogy with translation can be brought further through a reading prompted by Lory Chamberlain's article "Gender and the Metaphorics of Translation" (1992), here the male/female relationship is analyzed with reference to the control exercised on faithfulness and purity as pillars of patriarchal societies.

As the translator replaces the author in fathering the (female) text and takes on the latter's duty to structure it and protect its purity, so the explorer/cartographer, surrogating the divine author of nature's text, professes the faithfulness of his intersemiotic translation, at the same time laying the premises for protection against either "savage" customs or future rival incursions.

Hardly any attention, however, was paid to the fact that explorers were usually backed by institutions like the Royal Geographical Society or the colonial administration. Ryan analyses some of the instructions given to explorers and points out how pedantic they were as to what had to be observed and recorded – especially with reference to the indigenous population – even prescribing the kind of language to be used, a "close, naked, natural way of speaking" (1996, 39) which in its pursuit of objectivity had to refrain from elements typical of fiction and prefer the plain language of the middle class to the conceits of academics. In this perspective, the picture of the courageous individual devoted to widening knowledge fades into that of a civil servant paving the way for economic enterprise whose anxiety to be believed may mirror the ambiguity of the task undertaken. Within such parameters, explorers were entitled to absolute authority in naming and recording land features and impressions. The new world on which they set their gaze – new to Europeans, since most of these territories had obviously already been "discovered" by their inhabitants – was thus rewritten in Cartesian coordinates and incorporated into a system that by inscribing implied claiming rights. The choice to portray certain features and ignore others – among which contact with indigenous peoples and their relationship to the land – betrays, according to Ryan, a "failing to reflect the land and the empirical knowledge produced by exploration", with the result that at a political level maps are "an incitement to the alteration of ownership" (1996, 124).

Denying recognition to indigenous customs is a way to negate previous history and condition the present, leading to political and financial exploitation: in a series of talks on contemporary Canadian literature held at the University of Turin (Sep. 4-13, 2002), Richard Lane pointed out how First Nation people in British Columbia were, until the 1990s, repeatedly denied refund for the territories they had lost to imperial domination because, according to the courts, ownership had to be demonstrated through maps, and they could produce none. Similarly, only in the late 1980s, after legal battles involving the High Court, did the Meriam people in the Murray Islands receive compensation, denied before on the ground that the islands were considered waste lands of the Crown of Queensland. Both previous occupation of the land and the tradition of orally delimiting it by reference to natural landmarks (e.g. rocks, trees, springs) were dismissed as irrelevant and therefore ignored. Such cases illustrate (although in the negative) Ryan's definition of maps as "performative" in the sense in which the term is used in linguistics to designate "an utterance that effects an action by being spoken or by means of which the speaker performs a particular act" (*New Shorter OED*): maps are seen as texts able to modify or manipulate reality. The ability to negate a people's history owing to the absence of written records found theoretical support in Hegel's Philosophy of History, according to which "primitive", "undeveloped" African peoples were deemed unable to fix reality and hence to determine their own historical destiny; where writing was used, as in the East, its purport was neutralized through the construct of timelessness: imperishable, the Oriental world could be conquered and subjugated, but never energized from within. In both cases, the possibility of agency was erased so that the resulting passivity and backwardness justified the choice to ignore the past and henceforth record history as a linear teleological narrative brought in by the West.

Authorial descriptions gained more credibility through the explorer's admission of awe and speechlessness in front of new landscapes; words, however, normally did follow this initial incapability, with the result that the reader – having experienced the same astonishment – could not but appreciate the effort made to overcome it and depict the view. Standing for a guarantee of sincerity, a declaration of powerlessness helps the initial identification with the explorer and renders him more reliable in the reader's eyes; at the same time, as Ryan remarks, it makes use of a shared literary convention that works by "compartmentalizing the threatening within the sub-field of aesthetic perception called 'the sublime'" (1996, 84), thus including the taming of the new land in the pleasure given by a much sought-after – albeit finally reassuring – feeling of terror which further exalted the figure of the explorer. If the mode of description did not emphasize striking or wild features, it often made use of the cultural notion of the picturesque, whereby the eye caught – or produced – scenes possessing the elements or qualities of a picture, whose composition and colours afforded aesthetic pleasure. In its social significance, the picturesque is associated to the ownership of land and to a kind of landscape gardening that by moving trees, streamlets and hillocks, tries to reproduce a "natural" and pleasing effect. By taming nature, then, the representation in picturesque terms implied a prefiguration of ownership and hinted at the possibility of future human intervention.

The attribution of European toponyms to non-European places had the effect of naturalizing an otherwise foreign presence and creating outposts from which actual colonization could spread. At a discourse level, the mechanism at work in this case – often essentialist in its focussing on certain characteristics – could be termed synecdochical: by reproducing the same names (or adding the pre-modifier 'New') that identified cities, villages and areas in their home country, explorers took a part to signify the whole of the old world left behind, thereby transferring their cultural coordinates to the (no longer) foreign environment; the reassuring familiarity with their previous world was thus maintained and successfully combined with the promises of the new regions through an operation that transformed colonized territories into textual artefacts. Through this operation space was conceptualized into place: open, indefinite territories became physically delimited areas governed by rules and inhabited by Europeans. The symbolic link between old and new, here and there, affected both historical and spatial perception, so that the new territories came to represent peripheral extensions of Europe whose history was recorded according to Western canons, thereby highlighting only the events that followed the colonial encounter.

Pratt points out how the superscription of European textual elements on indigenous territories was further reinforced by the enormous impact of Carl von Linné's naturalistic classification, which further increased the notion of exploration as scientific progress based on neutral and objective criteria. The scientists of the time conceived of the world as chaos which their intervention could reorder:

> The eighteenth-century classificatory system created the task of locating every species on the planet, extracting it from its particular, arbitrary surroundings (the chaos), and placing it in its appropriate spot in the system (the order – book, collection, or garden) with its new, written, secular European name. (1992, 31)

Their aim therefore was not mimesis, but rather the creation of a rational framework in which to insert all flora, fauna and people. Naming played a fundamental role because it established new relationships and hierarchies, but it is impossible not to notice the tension between the Edenic figure of the name-giver and the total arbitrariness both of the word and of the category established. The narrativization of nature constituted the bulk of what Pratt terms "anti-conquest", that is, a naturalization of European bourgeois hegemonic presence represented as innocently engaged in gathering knowledge. Distance was levelled as natural elements found in very different parts of the world were united under homogeneous labels provided through a process of "global resemanticizing" (Pratt 1992, 31) that enriched and integrated maps, which came to provide information about the minerals, raw materials and animals to be found in different regions. As a result, coastal exploration evolved into a deeper and deeper movement towards the interior, and the number of travellers to the least known areas of the world increased dramatically: would-be botanists and entomologists eager to do their own sampling and categorizing went on their missions, while the easier location of resources gave new impetus to commercial exploitation, promoting a shift from a merchant system to a capitalistic one based on the exploitation of raw materials. The notion spread that those resources belonged to mankind and were wasted as, in terms of the values of the Western commercial and industrial system, nobody took advantage of them. Thus, even if aestheticized and mythologized, nature was unequal in distribution and it was (Western) humanity's task to restore the balance, while the implied accusation of laziness further aggravated the moral position of the indigenous population. Subsequently Darwinism, anthropology and ethnography, which in the same positivistic logic conceived of the world as a collection of things, looked at human beings as objects of study to be observed, measured and classified on the basis of an evolutionary ladder that depicted the various levels of advancement of peoples and viewed most extra-European societies as late exemplars of earlier developmental stages. Research and documentation justified voyeuristic scrutiny, especially of African women, while alleged phrenological evidence allowed for sweeping generalizations regarding cognitive abilities and moral attitudes of non-Europeans.

 A further incitement for Europeans to go and introduce their behavioural and moral models to their less lucky brethren came from religious writing. While the Christian vision that has all humans equal as children of God was difficult to reconcile with existing tropes of darker peoples being linked with the devil, positing them as children still lingering in an original sin condition allowed for convenient paternalistic missions to elevate them, and in so doing imbibe a patient acceptance in the hope of redemption that would help them conform to Western patterns. One of the most famous missionary hymns in English – *From Greenland's Icy Mountains* by Bishop Reginald Heber (discussed later in greater detail, given its reference to Sri Lanka) – was finally left out of Christian worship in the mid-twentieth-century owing to its embarrassing theological imperialism: the "heathens" were in fact depicted as begging the white man's intervention so as to be delivered from their sinful condition. Still adopted today both in economic and political matters to justify interference in other countries in the public's eyes, this strategy is identified by Spurr as an instance of "appropriation", which is "transformed into the response to an appeal from the colonized" (1993, 26).

Having looked at the most significant characteristics that – deliberately or not – inform exploration accounts and maps, it is interesting to notice that in spite of their sweeping popularity and influence, "traveller's tales" retain to this day the meaning of "incredible and probably untrue stories". Deep down, common sense might have kept a kind of filter, urging us to interrogate language and to remember that as a matter of fact these discourse operations and ideological constructs contradict the vision of language as divine, confirming on the contrary the arbitrariness of signs, which can be imposed by (any) man to denote – and create – reality. To say it in Ryan's words, "the form itself creates meaning" (1996, 105).

Literature, however, did not seem to question such attitudes. Post-colonial deconstructive analysis has demonstrated how by implicitly accepting the authority of travel journals and maps, British – and European – works often reflected and further consolidated a view that considered the rest of the world as extensions of the various imperial nations. Restricting the scope to English literature, many studies – among which notably Said's *Orientalism* and *Culture and Imperialism* – have pointed out how in many classics the perspectives presented through geographical notation and maps, as well as the underlying imperial relationships such texts reflected were taken for granted as scarcely visible yet well-established patterns of territorial control and economic exploitation that nurtured stability at home. Orientalism, according to Said, dates back to the end of the eighteenth century and is "the corporate institution for dealing with the Orient" (2003, 3), a body of knowledge that created an image of the East supporting Europe's expansion. Drawing on Karl Marx's statements on India's passivity, intricacies, superstition, lack of "known history",[4] orientalists elaborated an articulate representative discourse that through intellect and imagination constructed Europe's Other on the basis of binary oppositions among which male/female, civilized/savage, rational/irrational, active/passive. Works like *The Tempest, Robinson Crusoe, Jane Eyre, Great Expectations,* or even the seemingly unaffected *Mansfield Park,* have been re-read using the interpretative strategy that in *Culture and Imperialism* Said terms "contrapuntal reading, that is, an "effort to draw out, extend, give emphasis and voice to what is silent or marginally present or ideologically represented" (1993, 78), with the aim not only to study the Eurocentric assumptions such classics are based on, but also to expose the naturalness with which they perpetuated such visions. Beside the interest travel writing and cartography have awakened among post-colonial scholars, the *topos* of the map fascinates post-colonial writers, who are conjugating it in various ways with the aim of deconstructing, parodying and allegorizing Eurocentric visions. The recurrence of maps or of characters somehow engaged in reading, deciphering or reconstructing the land, either because of their profession or of circumstances, bears witness to a deeply felt, interrogative and provisional relationship with the natural environment. Also deployed as one of the expressions of post-colonial intertextuality, the rereading of cartography in fiction provides a means through which writers can disclose the dominant logic informing it and at the same time propose different types of spatial

---

[4] Marx wrote a series of articles on British rule in India published in *The New York Daily Tribune* in the summer of 1953.

coordinates. In their questioning or revising the existing literary canon, post-colonial writers are well aware of the tension between the map's prescriptive pretence of finiteness and inclusiveness and its inability to be totally comprehensive. In their revision of maps, they overcome the idea of a system of containment and adopt the position of the French post-structuralists Gilles Deleuze and Félix Guattari, who on the contrary highlight the openness of cartographical representations. Having identified different types of interconnections, Deleuze and Guattari postulate the ideal map as a rhizomatic text which spreads in all directions and assumes diverse forms, a text that can be connected at any point to anything other, and interrupted at a certain spot only to start up again without any significant loss or damage, but above all a text that develops at a horizontal level and not according to a power-determined hierarchical model. Such characteristics correspond to the way cognitive mapping works, and can be found in much post-colonial fiction with its cross-cultural perspectives, alternative spatial configurations, multiplicity of voices, parody of names, and its use of *bricolage* as a way to show the hybridity of existence and the impossibility to reduce it to a self-contained, linear representation.

1.1 Western Images of Sri Lanka

Silha, Taprobane, Zeilan, Ceylon... names replaced one another as explorers and traders from various countries touched the island. Although Macedonian, Greek, Roman and Arab traders gave accounts of their trips, this review will restrict itself to a few images provided by English writers to illustrate some of the textual strategies at work.

***

From Sir John Maundeville, *The voiage and travaile of Sir John Maundeville, Kt*:[5]

---

[5] Ed. James Orchard Halliwell-Phillipps, 1839. Reprint, London: F. S. Ellis, 1866.

Fro this Lond men gon to another yle, that is clept Silha: and it is welle a 800 Myles aboute. In that Lond is fulle mochelle waste; for it is fulle of Serpentes, of Dragouns, and of Cokadrilles; that no man dar duelle there. [...] And there ben also many wylde Bestes, and namelyche of Olyfauntes. In that yle is a gret Mountayne; and in mydd place of the Mount, is a gret Lake in a fulle faire Pleyne, and there is gret plentee of Watre. And thei of the Contree seyn, that Adam and Eve Wepten upon that Mount an 100 Zeer, whan thei weren dryven out of paradys. And that Watre, thei seyn, is of here Teres: for so moche Watre thei wepten, that made the forseyde Lake. And in the botme of that Lake, men fynden many precious Stones and grete Perles. (1866, 198-199)

[...]

Toward the Est partye of Prestre Johnes Lond, is an Yle gode and gret, that men clepen Taprobane, that is fulle noble, and fulle fructuous: and the Kyng thereof is fulle ryche, and is undre the obeyssance of Prestre John. And alle weys there thei make hire Kyng be Eleccyoun. In that Ile ben 2 Someres and 2 Wyntres: and men hervesten the Corn twyes a Zeer. And in alle the Cesouns of the Zeer ben the Gardynes florisht. There dwellen gode folk and resonable, and manye Cristene men amonges hem, that ben so riche that thei wyte not what to done with hire Godes. (1866, 300)

Taprobane, the Greek and Latin name for Sri Lanka, meant "the garden of delights", a land of imagination full of promise to Europeans, who learnt about its wealth and allure mainly through the fourteenth-century travel book by Sir John Maundeville and Marco Polo's *Journeys in the Island of Zeilan*. The double reference in Maundeville's account, Silha and Taprobane, the alleged presence of fabulous beasts, and the terms of his description give the account the quality of a mythological journey mixed with Christian themes. Moving gradually closer, the perspective narrows from the outline of the island to the wilderness and, having overcome its dangers, to the mountain which is presented in both cases as a garden of Eden, linked to Paradise through Adam and Eve's fall, thus a place where sinners can find redemption and, interestingly, pearls and precious stones. The reference to one of the fundamental Christian motifs renders the exotic foreignness of the island reassuring, while there seems to be an implicit suggestion that the treasures found at the bottom of the lake are also the fruit of repenting tears to which Christians might have full title. Adam and Eve crying for one hundred years, moreover, imply a monogenistic vision that allows the writer to positively highlight signs of civilization such as the election of the king and cultivation of the land. At the same time, however, the emphasis on abundance and riches casts an ambiguous light on the inhabitants, who have more than is necessary and do not know how to use it. The image, which became a recurrent way of justifying European appropriation, was bound to arouse guilt-free desire, especially in the turbulent and plagued England of the late fourteenth century.

***

Reginald Heber, "From Greenland's Icy Mountains", 1819.[6]

> From Greenland's icy mountains,
> From India's coral strand;
> Where Afric's sunny fountains
> Roll down their golden sand;
> From many an ancient river,
> From many a palmy plain,
> They call us to deliver
> Their land from error's chain!
> What though the spicy breezes

---

[6] In *The Poetical Works of Reginald Heber* (Philadelphia: E. H. Butler & Co., 1858).

Blow soft o'er Ceylon's isle;
Though every prospect pleases,
And only man is vile:
In vain with lavish kindness
The gifts of God are strown;
The heathen in his blindness
Bows down to wood and stone!
Can we, whose souls are lighted
With Wisdom from on high,
Can we to men benighted
The lamp of life deny?
Salvation! Oh, Salvation!
The joyful sound proclaim,
Till each remotest nation
Has learn'd Messiah's name!
Waft, waft, ye winds, His story,
And you, ye waters, roll,
Till like a sea of glory,
It spreads from pole to pole!
Till o'er our ransom'd nature
The Lamb for sinners slain,
Redeemer, King, Creator,
In bliss returns to reign!
(1858, 264-265)

Besides resting on overt prejudice, Bishop Heber's joyful and benign hymn, often quoted in nineteenth-century memoirs and travel journals, reveals itself as a product of less immediate cultural bias. With the accumulation of geographical names, the opening verses create an almost circular emitting frame whose unnamed – and yet obvious – centre and intended receiver is Europe, further confirmed in its vantage point by the use of "from" to indicate the direction in which the appeals move. The exotic synecdoches paint an attractive panorama against which the callers are finally projected (and easily imagined red, yellow and black, according to the race classifications of the time) in a timeless request that clearly distinguishes "them" from "us". Heber, Bishop of Calcutta with authority over Ceylon too, refers to the fabled island as a land of the imagination[7] where soft breezes blow the scent of its much sought-after spices. No longer the good Christian people of Maundeville, its inhabitants are now base, in striking contrast to the wisdom received from "on high" by the Europeans, who cannot refrain from the moral duty to bring light to those still erring in darkness, a pattern that corresponds to what Thomas Docherty labels "apocalyptic" narrative (1996, 62), that is, proceeding from mystification to enlightenment and revelation. Interestingly, as Ryan points out, "prospect" is the result of the action of looking out into space, but also of looking forward into time, which, considering the hint at commercial goods, adds teleological intentionality to an already captivating description. Having stated the problem and given the solution, Heber commands praise to the Lord till His name is learnt by even the "remotest nations" and His story is spread "from pole to pole", strengthening this domineering envisaging of Western religious colonization through the image of a "ransomed", unified world. It is "our" nature, however, that reveals a more mundane aspect: be it the physical environment or human nature, once ransomed it goes – or is restored – to Europe.

***

From Henry Marshall, *Ceylon: A General Description of the Island and Its Inhabitant*:[8]

---

[7] Heber wrote the hymn in 1819, but only in 1925 did he go to Ceylon. Based on hearsay and on collective images of the Orient, the hymn was even temporarily changed to portray Java instead of Ceylon for metrical reasons, which reveals the generalizing attitude of exotic constructs.

[8] London: William H. Allen and Co., 1846.

Immediately upon reaching the summit of the Peak, the senior priest waited upon us, and made many inquiries respecting our health, &c. Having learned that we intended to remain there all night, he most earnestly recommended and entreated us to alter our determination in that respect; he said we should certainly be visited with sickness if we remained on the hill all night. As he found our resolution to remain in his neighbourhood was not to be altered, he disappeared, but in a very short time returned, bringing with him a handful of dried plants, [...] an amulet. (1846, 236-237)

[...]

An opinion prevails amongst the natives of Ceylon, that no one but a priest can reside with impunity even for a night on the Peak, [...] disease or death being the penalties to which it is said transgressors are liable. [...] In consequence of this delusion, it was with much difficulty that Mr. Sawers prevailed upon his servants and followers to remain on the Peak all night. Being unprovided with any accommodation, it must be admitted that they were exposed to much discomfort, and a degree of cold not known in Ceylon except in a similar situation. (1846, 237-238)

[...]

It would be in vain for me to attempt to describe the beauty of the magnificent scene which engaged our attention for a great part of the time we were on the Peak. On each side of the mountain we gazed with delight over an irregular surface of mountains, hills, and ridges, covered with trees and foliage, variously coloured with different shades of brown, green and red. Tropical forests have always an autumnal appearance,

1 Cartography and Mapping 27

probably from the constant reproduction and decay of the foliage. [...]

Towards sunset, our attention was much directed to the rapid formation of clouds, and to their seemingly fantastical changes in appearance and rapid motions.

[...]

The moon shone bright, while the clouds were at rest, apparently reposing on the surface of the earth, presenting a uniform stratum of the finest down or rather snow [...] If the reader can imagine a pure white sea, interspersed with a number of densely-wooded and dark-coloured islands, some idea may be formed of the moonlight view we enjoyed. (1846, 238)

Henry Marshall served in Ceylon from 1809 to 1821 as surgeon to the 1st and 2nd Ceylon Regiments, and subsequently published the account of his experience in London in 1846. In the introduction to the 1982 Sri Lankan edition the book is praised as "invaluable for a study [...] of the events which preceded and followed the conquest of the Kandyan Kingdom" and for its "unprejudiced accounts of the laws, customs, religion and political and social structure of the Kandyan Kingdom" (1982, i). It opens in a taxonomic mode, dividing observations into short sections titled "Situation, Extent, Physical Aspect", "Soil, Agriculture, &c.", "Animals", "Inhabitants", often subdivided into more specific paragraphs. The bulk of the book is its "Historical Sketch", dealing briefly with the Portuguese and Dutch conquests and devoting a much longer part to British attempts to seize coastal Ceylon first and then the central Kandyan region. The excerpts quoted are included in the appendixes, a sundry collection of journal-like reports, conventions, letters and official declarations, and relate how "Mr. Sawers, the Commissioner of Revenue in the Kandyan provinces, and the writer of these pages" went on an expedition to Ceylon's highest mountain, Adam's Peak. The account belongs to the type termed by Gérard Genette "subsequent narrative", which implies the use of the past tense and a narration from an advanced temporal point, though it is highly likely that notes had been taken at the time. It must be said that some of the uneasiness Marshall felt in his career as a colonialist surfaces in the text, where the prevailing European rhetoric and conventions reveal every now and then quasi-comical or disturbing subtexts. In an instance of the attitude that opposes an undifferentiated mass of natives to the vigorous explorer, the party is said to have consisted of about eighty or ninety between "coollies who carried the tent, chair-bearers, baggage-coollies, servants, &c." (1982, 171), but the expectation of the two Englishmen "that the road would permit of our being carried in a chair" reduces considerably their adventurous aura. A more dignified balance is restored, however, upon learning that the luxuriant vegetation and the ruggedness of the road compel them to climb on foot. The difficulties of the ascent being overcome, the summit is reached, and the two excursionists, though aware of the sacredness of the mountain and its importance to many religions, choose not to heed the request of the custodian priest dismissing it as a delusion. Probably unwillingly, the text shows the difference in attitude to fellow human beings: while the defeated priest provides the trespassers with a protective amulet, they not only oblige the "natives" to go against their creed, but in so doing carelessly expose them to the cold that in all likelihood they see as the cause of "disease or death"; the comforting safety offered by the tent, by contrast, allows the (here etymologically true) travellers to indulge in the beauty of the spot, which is described in the most rapturous terms. The apologetic prelude about the impossibility to find words is followed by a detailed example of the verbal painting so common in Romantic and Victorian travel writing, with a privileged panoramic gaze that positions the viewer as central and enables him to comprehend his surroundings with the utmost accuracy. While the whole of the depiction elaborates on colours, shapes and movements conjuring a picturesque and uncanny image, it is worth noting that Marshall adopts the technique of deferral, whereby the landscape acquires substance and visibility insofar as it reminds of familiar European scenes. Hence the "autumnal appearance" of forests that because of their latitude do not know any autumn, the "snow" created by moonlight, and the summarizing dream-like simile – alterity reduced to identity in a vision shared with the reader in order to convince him or her that, as John Donne said, "the Eye is the location of truth".

***

From Frederick Lewis, *Sixty-four Years in Ceylon*:[9]

> My object in writing this book has been to give the simple story of a man's life in one of our Empire's Colonies, under conditions that may be regarded as exceptional, though possibly not unique.
>
> In my case, although I was born in an atmosphere of rigid British ideas; ideas that made me feel, as thorough a Briton as if I had never been out of England, yet I lived in a climate that was tropical; surrounded with all the contracting influences, that unconsciously, or subconsciously, become Colonial; uneducated, untamed, and with nothing to back me, pecuniary or otherwise, – these influences, in the aggregate, were bound to produce peculiar ideas of life, and angles of observation, completely different from those of our home-born countrymen.
>
> My early struggles and handicaps, aroused in me strange lines of thought and a life-long feeling of shyness of my

---

[9] Colombo: Colombo Apothecaries Co., 1923.

fellow-creatures. That feeling, makes me wonder to-day, how my fellow-creatures will accept this simple story.

I hope, that in their natural generosity, they will make allowances for my shortcomings, or for my narrowness of vision. I hope they will observe that my observations are made with no unkindly spirit, even though I have had to paint more than one character in dark colours, but with an honest desire to tell the truth, as the truth appeared to me. (1926, Preface)

[...]

I was born in Kandy on the 18th of July, 1858, in a small house in Trincomalee Street, that once formed a sort of supplement to an hotel that existed in those days. This house in later years was completely altered, and to-day [1923] has passed into one of the many native shops, in a form that renders it impossible to recognise it from any of its neighbours of a like character. (1926, 1)

[...]

After my birth, I was taken to the Mahaberiatenna Estate, and my first memories are associated with coffee estates, and the lonely life the planters endured in those days. (1926, 2)

[...]

In those days we lived an isolated kind of life, – that is to say no Europeans lived close at hand, but then, as ever in Ceylon, the planter's bungalow was always an open house.

Anybody on the way to, or from Kandy, to Rangalla, wishing to break their journey would come to our bungalow...(1926, 3)

[...]

In those days, Kandy was the main centre of the planting activity, The railway had not reached the planting capital, but the main difficulty in the way of determination of trace, and object to be attained, had been overcome.

The first section of the railway, as far as Ambepussa had been opened, thus lessening the toil in olden days of coaching the whole way to Colombo. With this great stride in the advancement of the Colony's interests, Ceylon's chief industry was practically bound up. (1926, 4)

[...]

Our nearest neighbours were planters, and many of them came to the country on the mere chance of employment. Naturally the class of men was variable in the extreme, but one and all enjoyed a great characteristic in common, – that of open hearted friendship and hospitality. [...] There was a spirit of trustfulness that made us all friends and a neighbourliness that made us all of one family, so to speak. Moreover, there was no such thing as distrusting your fellow whiteman; or secretly watching his method of work. The planting community was a happy family, each willing and ready to help the other to the full, and the best of his ability.

The relation between the planter and the cooly was remarkable. The cooly, to use his own apt phrase, looked on his "Dorey" as his "father and mother", and came to him in all his troubles and domestic difficulties. If he were sick the "Dorey" would cure him; if there was a dispute, the "Dorey" would enquire and probably thrash the wrong doers soundly. The "Master" was supreme in the coolies' eyes, and so he was in reality. I am not exaggerating when I say that coolies loved their masters, and would go to the world's end for them. [...] and faith went a long way with those good, child-like, honest people. (1926, 5-6)

[...]

The conditions of life which I have here briefly, and indifferently, tried to illustrate, naturally exercised a peculiar effect on the lives and temperament of the Europeans of that day. Men regarded themselves as very supreme and any interference with their systems of control was naturally repugnant to them. (1926, 6)

[...]

Obviously this course could not go on indefinitely: a day must come when a co-ordination of administration must come about. Any change that touched the planter, was bound to arouse comment, hostile or otherwise. Nor can this be wondered at, when men were to all intents and purposes, little kings within their own limited kingdoms. Here, therefore, consciously or unconsciously, was planted a seed that grew up into a mighty tree, unlike all others in the garden, and its fruits were not palatable to all alike. The planting community looked upon the Government as an unsympathetic and ignorant, dogmatic, master, incapable alike of understanding the planting interests, or of the people, with whom the planters were in constant touch. (1926, 6-7)

[...]

Estates were opened in all directions, labour was plentiful and cheap, and land was available that was adapted to the staple industry of the country. As a proof of this, it may be mentioned in passing, that out of a total of 33,451 acres of land sold in 1860, no less than 14,755 acres were sold in the Central Province alone.

In the same year (1860) what was regarded as a great want was the completion and construction of an iron lattice bridge over the Mahaweliganga at Katugastotta. A Ball was given, at which the Governor, and some two hundred and fifty persons were present. [...] The railway had been inaugurated two years previously, and was in course of construction, ant the country was well launched by this time upon a prosperous career. (1926, 7)

In his autobiographical narrative, Frederick Lewis voices some of the anxiety and attitudes that informed British imperialism and gives representations of space that, while perpetuating a well-established tradition, also signal a furthering of the colonial enterprise. The Preface shows an instance of the widespread practice of colonial discourse that established a connection between moral standing and the climatic environment whereby northern climates allegedly foster diligence and self-control, while the heat of the tropics induces indolence and an easy or excessive sexuality. In an apologetic tone Lewis explains how, in spite of his rigid British education, the tropical environment transformed him into a colonial, thus separating him from his countrymen born in the motherland, and determined a feeling of inferiority that only the latter's openmindedness was able to excuse. Caught between the authority provided by his own experience and social position in the colony and the inadequacy he fears, Lewis resorts to a conventional profession of truth, significantly questioned immediately after by his remark "as the truth appeared to me."

Hardly the heroic male figures of old, planters are described drawing on the one hand on the nobilitating convention of loneliness, hardship and individual enterprise, and on the other in an almost pietistic tone that celebrates the happy, open community loved by their servants. The Ceylon presented through Lewis' words bears no resemblance to the mysterious and alluring depictions of the first explorers; rather, it is a utilitarian gaze that looks at the transformations regretting the fact that his birth-house – converted into a "native shop" – can no longer be distinguished from others. The nostalgic complaint fails to recognize how the Western superimposition both erased meaningful symbolic places belonging to a pre-existing culture and determined a dramatic acceleration in the whole system of life, whose most evident manifestation was the construction of the railway. The picturesque used to prefigure ownership and exploitation of the land has given way to geographical notations that reflect the achievements or the prospects of economic development: places are mentioned insofar as they pertain to the planting activity, an aspect that matches the imprinting deriving from the author's infancy on coffee estates. Thus, of Kandy the reader only learns that it was "the centre of the planting activity", and that the journey to Colombo had been somewhat eased by a railway stretch up to Ambepussa. Lewis does not question the legitimacy of the land being increasingly sold to incoming settlers, land that – it is worth pointing out – the British had conquered in 1815 following the defeat of the Kandyan Kingdom with the pretext of delivering the inhabitants from a barbarous king. The native people being then deprived of their land and becoming "plentiful and cheap labour" subjected to "little kings within their own limited kingdoms" do not stir Lewis' conscience nor seem to contradict the frequently quoted civilizing mission of the white men (whose real motivation was "the mere chance of employment"), as the "coolies" developed towards them a faithful and affectionate relationship. The account mixes traits of scientific and sentimental writing, where the emphasis on cultivation and land measurements mixes with the author's own experiences, memories and desires; moreover, the condescending attitude towards the indigenous population confirms Pratt's observation about the use of sentimental stereotypes to describe a people after they have been totally subdued.

***

Sentimental and orientalist traits also combine in some of Leonard Woolf's writings on Sri Lanka. The following passage, taken from the short story "A Tale Told by Moonlight",[10] postulates the East as the place where the Englishman can experience life to the full, in those extreme manifestations that the civilized metropolis does not provide. The Orient is perceived through smells, fleetingly caught through one half of a bizarre door, heard in the sound of bare feet and finally touched and dived into in its representation of naked or half-clad female bodies joyfully welcoming the foreigners.

> Well, he wanted to see life, to understand it, to feel it. He had travelled 7000 miles to do so. He was very keen to begin, he wanted to see life all round, up and down, inside and out; he told me so as we looked out on the palm trees and the glimpse of the red road beyond and the unending stream of brown men and women upon it. (1962, 259)
>
> [...]
>
> We bowled along the dusty roads past the lake and into the native quarter. All the smells of the East rose up and hung heavy upon the damp hot air in the narrow streets. [. . .]
>
> There was one of those queer native wooden doors made in two halves; the top half was open and through it one saw an empty white-washed room lighted by a lamp fixed in the wall. We went in and I shut the door top and bottom behind us. At the other end were two steps leading up to another room. Suddenly there came the sound of bare feet running and giggles of laughter, and ten or twelve girls, some naked and some half clothed in bright red or bright orange clothes,

---

[10] In Leonard Woolf, *Diaries in Ceylon 1908-1911: Records of a Colonial Administrator & Stories from the East* (London: Hogarth Press, 1962).

rushed down the steps upon us. We were surrounded, embraced, caught up in their arms and carried into the next room. We lay upon sofas with them. There was nothing but sofas and an old piano in the room.

They knew me well in the place – you can imagine what it was – I often went there. Apart from anything else, it interested me. The girls were all Tamils and Sinhalese. It always reminded me somehow of the Arabian Nights; that room when you came into it so bare and empty, and then the sudden rush of laughter, the pale yellow naked women, the brilliant colours of the cloths, the white teeth, all appearing so suddenly in the doorway up there at the end of the room. And the girls themselves interested me; I used to sit and talk to hem for hours in their own language; they didn't as a rule understand English. They used to tell me all about themselves, queer pathetic stories often. They came from villages almost always, little native villages hidden far away among rice fields and coconut trees, and they had drifted somehow into this hovel in the warren of filth and smells which we and our civilization had attracted about us. (1962, 259-260)

The beautification of the scene is carried on through the pleasure evoked by the furniture and the reference to the *Arabian Nights*, and further enhanced by the colours used to describe the women, their clothes, their teeth, in a resulting atmosphere of harmony that obliterates the much less poetic reality of a brothel. The quasi-scientific interest the narrator insists upon, both in the place and the girls, could be looked at as symbolic of the attitude of European colonizers toward foreign lands and people, where the exploitative relationship is hidden behind allegedly humane behaviour on one side and complacent availability on the other. Pratt notices how sentimental travel writing converts women both for domestic and sexual work "into the beneficent female figure of the 'nurturing native' who tends to the suffering European out of pity, spontaneous kindness or erotic passion" (1992, 96). The passage also reminds of Gobineau's theory according to which the white races felt a civilizing instinct that forced them to "mix their blood with that of others" (Young 1995, 108) in an effort to regenerate inferior or degenerate races; the noble impetus of the whites, then, contains in itself the flaw that will determine their own decadence: adulteration of the race in the case of children born of mixed-race marriages, or, in fictional terms, unhappy endings usually consisting of separation of the lovers, return of the European to his homeland and early death of the native woman, which is what happens here.

In spite of the praise received by many non-European critics, according to Minoli Samarakkody (1997), Woolf's writing is heavily conditioned by Orientalism and his belief in the civilizing mission of colonialism. While Samarakkody's critique does not concede much to Woolf's growing disbelief in the system, which would eventually prompt him to resign from the Ceylon Civil Service, it is difficult not to notice that the treatment of indigenous characters ranges from masses of backdrop-like brown people to individuals described through a multitude of references to their animal qualities, stressing in the case of women their voluptuousness, passivity and dependency.

> He was a civilized cultivated intelligent nervous little man and she – she was an animal, dumb and stupid and beautiful.
>
> [...] she had grown to love him, love him like an animal, as a bitch loves her master.
>
> [...]
>
> It's the love of a slave, the patient, consuming love for a master, for his kicks and his caresses, for his kisses and his blows. (1962, 263)

The Orient, then, represents also in Woolf the place where man, inebriated with sensuality, falls prey to illusions and loses himself.

> And when he looked into her patient, mysterious eyes, he saw behind them what he had fallen in love with, what he knew didn't exist. It began to drive him mad. (*ibid.*)

The mystery of the Orient pervades Sri Lanka and finds its greatest location in the jungle, which defies description and inscription through its perennial and yet self-renovating nature. Woolf's fascination with the jungle can be perceived in his *Diaries in Ceylon 1908-1911* and more so in *The Village in the Jungle* (1913), where his fondness for the rural district of Hambantota seems to derive primarily from the wildness of the place, mainly described through absence.

> Born and bred in London, I was a little surprised by the primitive conditions of life in the Ceylon of those days. It took me over two days to get from Colombo to Jaffna. The first day I went by train to Anuradhapura, where I had to spend the night. The railway line ended at Anuradhapura, and I had to go by coach from Anuradhapura to Elephant Pass. The coach was simply a bullock cart and the passengers sat or lay on the tappal bags. (*Diaries*, 1962, lxxv)

> [...]

> I had come to Ceylon in a state of political innocence, for I had never really considered what my relations would be with the inhabitants of the Island. I now found myself in the position of an empire-builder and imperialist, and it was in Jaffna that I first became dimly aware of the problems – and to me personal problems – of imperialism. (1962, lxxvi)

> [...]

> I was nearly three years in Hambantota as Assistant Government Agent. I grew to be extremely fond of the place and its people. It was pure Sinhalese, no planters, no Europeans at all except a District Judge in Tangalla, two Irrigation Engineers, and an Assistant Superintendent of Police. It was entirely rural and agricultural in the west, and a vast stretch of jungle with the game sanctuary in the east. There were no real towns, no railway, hardly any roads. [...] The impact of my experiences during those years was powerful. I was fascinated and deeply moved by the lives of the villagers and their psychology, and also by the perpetual menace of nature, the beautiful and at the same time sinister and savage life of the jungle. (1962, lxxvii-lxxviii)

By first subtracting the white man and then the signs of his presence – towns, railway, roads – Woolf seems to be erasing elements of the landscape in a sort of "verbal unpainting" that in the eyes of the reader reduces place to space and perpetuates essentialist binarisms like Sinhalese/European and nature/civilization. The focus, however, is the jungle, which in the last paragraph in the quote arches over the quasi-ethnographic gaze sweeping on the villagers only in relation to the reaction produced on the observer and reducing them to the role of extras on the sublime stage: it is not so much their life *in* it, but rather the life *of* the jungle itself – threatening, beautiful, and sinister – that interests the chronicler.

2 The Making of History

Mutually constitutive, geography and history intertwine and depend on each other for further consolidation and development. Thus, according to Paul Carter (1987), newly attributed geographical names bring history into being in that, through them, space is transformed into place and defined in terms of coordinates within which history can manifest itself, while history in turn naturalizes the territorial divisions and formations thus created and "institutionalizes forgetfulness of earlier territorializations in the perception of the world" (Rabasa in Ashcroft *et al.* 1995, 362).

The rationale for history lies in the desire to record the past so as to learn from it, as well as in the establishment of a tradition of constant evolution of a people that helps define its identity and the direction it moves in. While in its humanistic conception history belongs to those human endeavours to give systematic form to knowledge and to weave far-reaching, comprehensive models to make sense of life, contemporary criticism is well aware of its deep political implications and of the role it plays in determining present and future actions.

In the West, history is inextricably linked with writing, as this is traditionally considered the means through which it can come into existence and meet the necessary requirements to gain the value of truth (which is what prompted Hegel to claim in *The Philosophy of History* that Africa's reliance on orality condemned it to a position outside history). The assumption is that the records of past events can be ordered into a continuous linear perspective that provides interpolation for the missing "evidence", so that the links between significant stages of development will be automatically revealed. In this sense, history appears to adjust itself, sometimes even "transforming in retrospect the incredible into the inevitable" (Sarvan 1995, 65), a contention that aptly describes the impression often derived when reading history texts that events unfold before one's eyes without the intervention of any author. However, growing doubts have been raised about the positivist idea that the real is reached through its own representation and that realistic writing objectively encapsulates truth. Therefore, historical discourse has increasingly been looked at as one of many verbal artefacts stemming, like others, from ideologies that Hayden White defines as "contemplative" or "manipulative" depending respectively on their acceptance of the *status quo* or, conversely, on a desire to express criticism in order to transform or eliminate existing structures (1990, 68). According to this view, historical discourse appears to be an interpretation of past events, the result of the historian's choice to compress or elide certain aspects and to expand others. Hence, a similarity is postulated between historical writing and storytelling, as the "fictions of factual representation" (1990, 121) so obtained rely on tropes that "*constitute* the objects which [discourse] pretends only to describe realistically and to analyze objectively" (1990, 2).

In order to guarantee a "true" and objective account, the centres where history is produced (typically the academia) draw on historiographic sources like administrative papers, graphs, laws and other documents, which state the primacy of the written word over any other kind of memory. Documents are certainly tested for authenticity and reliability, but the distance in time is bound to raise doubts as often the material referent no longer exists, so that value is ascertained on the surface of texts according to their conformity to the rules and conventions that in a given society, in a given chronological and spatial framework, constitute the code of truthfulness. Pasco (2004) points out a growing trend among historians to adduce novels, poems, and plays as illustrations and sources. This stance has generated the criticism of those who, following Plato, believe art is a lie, but has also met the favour of historians who agree that, even if literary works are not fact, they do provide useful insight into the attitudes, states of mind, prejudices and emotions of the people living in a certain era, thus revealing aspects to which one rarely has access as they were probably recorded in private letters and diaries hardly filed as archival material.

The debate around the foundations and practices of history has been enriched by the contribution of the Popular Memory Group, based at the University of Birmingham, who have been exploring the possibility of becoming "historians of the present too" (1982, 208). Building on the limits and contradictions of academic history, they point out that the documents it is reconstructed upon are "records of authority" (1982, 216) – which, although unchallenged because of their institutional origin, do not dispel disturbing doubts about their potentially biased perspective and/or instrumental interpretation to construct a certain reality – and propose integrating them with popular autobiography and community-shared experience generated through recourse to memory and orality, so that both official representations and private consciousness will be included in the way the past is presented to society. Outside academia, the explicit task of producing a version of "dominant memory" (often the result of struggles between competing representations of the past) is carried out by agencies connected – to a greater or lesser extent – to institutions, which create a more immediate public sense of history through state visits, military parades, commemorative celebrations and historical recreations. Often widely covered by the media, these events enter everyday life and represent in the eyes of many concrete manifestations of history, the perpetuation of traditions through which one's identity is also shaped. Slightly less institutional, but still linked to the state or the local government, are those bodies which operate in the educational and preservation fields, like schools, museums, art galleries, archives of various kinds and the wide range of initiatives going under the heading "national heritage", which strengthen pride in and a sense of belonging to a specific cultural and historical space. Moreover, the fascination with history has percolated into business, concretizing itself in publishing (many "historical" best-sellers are biographies, autobiographies, military histories and romance portrayals of epochs or charismatic figures), cinema, and so-called cultural tourism, whereby historically significant sites and buildings are commodified into resources for the leisure and tourist industries. Finally, the media play a major role as a source of history-making in that they not only select particular aspects to be highlighted in retrospective through documentaries, special features or drama, but also produce day by day the contemporary history that emerges from piecing together journalistic news that, by convention, are expected to be grounded in actuality, localized in time and place, metonymic and referential, and therefore *a priori* conferred a particular position that does not even contemplate the need for the suspension of disbelief fiction proper demands. The collective sense of history is thus mainly shaped through a narration that, in spite of the variety of means of which it avails itself, tends to produce a univocal shared past formalized in the concept of "nation", thereby allowing definition of self by contrast with what is external and therefore "Other".

However, as the reason for history lies not so much in fixing the past, but rather in revealing its relations to the present, it must be accepted that historical knowledge is also constantly produced in everyday talk and personal narratives, it finds substantiation in private letters, diaries and photo albums and can even develop into myth when an anecdote, for example, is spread among growing numbers of people. It is this kind of material that, like women's and working class history, tends to be submerged into silence as it hardly ever gains access to publicity. Hence, although aware of the danger represented by the selectivity of memory and the inevitably circumscribed point of view of the witness, the Popular Memory Group postulate the need for subjective experience to be collected and given a voice, contending that even the tiniest personal narrative is bound to be the product of interactions between the individual, the social body and more codified historical knowledge, and therefore an expression of both single insights and – taken together – of the collective consciousness at a given time. Including such sources implies the adoption of different methods, a change in the work of the historian – who would then be "in the field" and not dealing with inert material – but above all it means adding a democratic dimension and an alternative viewpoint from below, so that, as Antonio Gramsci argued, the newly acquired awareness of collective weaknesses, strengths and struggles in those who were excluded from the process will endow them with a greater transformative potential in society.

Such criticism of history has been influenced by the same broadly speaking deconstructionist readings recently applied to the humanities, although the main modes of investigation are inspired by previous instruments of analysis, namely those brought forth by the Bakhtin school with its belief that language cannot be separated from ideology and realizes in discourse the site for class struggle; by Marxist critics, for whom the relations of dominance and subordination informing the social and economic order of a certain phase of human history in some sense determine the whole cultural life of a society, and by the structuralist assumption that "the structure of a language produces 'reality'" (Selden 1985, 68).

Further interrogation of the whole Western system of thought came from Jacques Derrida, in whose opinion discourse always presupposes a centre, or point of origin, which is above and beyond scrutiny. Such logocentrism establishes the truth and consciousness that underwrite Western literature, history, theology and science and it is difficult to dismantle, as any attack generated in response to it acknowledges it and immediately substitutes a new centre for the old, with the result that the terms of the system are shifted but not changed.

A similar contention comes from Michel Foucault, who sees the anonymous, quasi-Kafkaesque net of relations that constitute power as aimed at growth and self-perpetuation, so that human history does not progress toward emancipation, but goes from domination to domination in a cyclical process. Foucault envisages power as percolating downward from the institutions positioned at the top of an imaginary pyramid, with knowledge operating as its instrument and finding its concrete realization in discourse. If discourse, then, is the site of domination in society, the critic is urged to engage in a complex relation with the text since, besides being part of a much more extensive framework made of other texts, institutions and practices, it is also backed – to a greater or lesser degree – by a political consciousness and therefore bound to have political impact. It is not only what is on the surface, but rather the silences and exclusions, the implicit hierarchies of values and the filiations of inter- and extratextuality that allow the text(ure) to emerge and the connections with the intellectual and material context to be revealed. Thus, reading follows the lines of archaeology – a synchronic investigation of the implicit rules of formation that condition the existence of every discourse as to its content and its expressive means – and of genealogy, a diachronic approach aimed at showing how every discourse has its roots in others, thereby undermining the absolutism of originality and self-naturalizing historical formations, even at the risk of seeming nihilist and relativist. The materials that constitute the historical archive – documents, models of economic growth, demographic statistics – allow analysts to identify various sedimentary strata, so that the traditionally researched linear successions have given way to discoveries in depth. Western history was characterized by attention to long periodizations in which events followed one another according to a logic of cause and effect in an attempt to reconstruct continuity and evolution along lines supposedly leading toward human progress. In *The Archaeology of Knowledge* (1972; 2004), Foucault highlights those underlying histories not prone to rapid changes and not featuring in historical narratives: "the history of sea routes, the history of corn or of gold-mining, the history of drought and of irrigation, the history of crop rotation, the history of the balance achieved by the human species between hunger and abundance" (2004, 4). As attention is increasingly turning to the inclusion of such information, new models of relations must be contemplated between them, accommodating the possibilities of "hierarchy, dominance, stratification, univocal determination, circular causality" (*ibid.*). Conversely, in other humanistic fields the focus has been moving away from vast wholes to instances of rupture and discontinuity, whereby a society, an artistic current or a scientific development gains depth in its portrayal not through its own – or superimposed – unifying elements, but through interruptions. The visualization of the past, then, is no longer a continuous line, but a cluster of interacting or parallel entities, whose limits define and transform each other, thereby creating ever new foundations.

Whether looking for overarching visions or for margins, historians have to engage with documents, and it is in this domain that a big change has manifested itself, for while the traditional attitude involved interpreting them and ascertaining their truthfulness in order to reconstruct that past of which they were a product, the current position is that of working from inside: "History now organizes the document, divides it up, distributes it, orders it, arranges it in levels, establishes series, distinguishes between what is relevant and what is not, discovers elements, defines unities, describes relations" (2004, 7). Unities, series, relations are looked for within the document itself, which comes to embody a microcosm of those social and cultural practices it emerged from, so that the history thus produced is redefined as "one way in which a society recognizes and develops a mass of documentation with which it is inextricably linked" (*ibid.*). Therefore, whereas the primary concern was to order the consequentiality of events and show their relation, the task now is to recreate each series in all its specificity of boundaries, chronologies and governing laws and then to reveal the relations between series, thus originating layers of historical narratives intersecting, overlapping and often moving in different directions which do not allow for totalities or teleological accounts.

Thus, in place of the continuous chronology of reason, which was invariably traced back to some inaccessible origin, there have appeared scales that are sometimes very brief, distinct from one another, irreducible to a single law, scales that bear a type of history peculiar to each one, and which cannot be reduced to the general model of a consciousness that acquires, progresses, and remembers. (2004, 9)

What the traditional historian perceived as an obstacle and tried to overcome – that is, discontinuity – is now integrated as a deliberate object of research because of the possibilities it opens by revealing the limits and contradictions of a given event or process. As a consequence of these changes, claims Foucault, history is no longer envisaged or desired as "total" – and therefore aiming to "reconstitute the overall form of a civilization" on the assumption of homogeneous relations and rational causality applicable to the various fields of human experience, from economics to technology, from social behaviour to moral – but as an investigative process yielding the possibility of a "general" history, one that problematizes and tries to legitimately describe the relations of simultaneity, dominance, correlation or other between different series constituted by religion, institutions, economy or literature:

> A total description draws all phenomena around a single centre – a principle, a meaning, a spirit, a world-view, an overall shape; a general history, on the contrary, would deploy the space of a dispersion. (2004, 11)

The evolution the new vision of history is undergoing is also defined through methodological issues. In fact, although some of them are by no means innovative (Foucault acknowledges Marx's fundamental contribution to epistemological mutation), taken together as an approach, they characterize it. Research tools are manifold:

> [. . .] the building-up of coherent and homogeneous corpora of documents (open or closed, exhausted or inexhaustible

corpora), the establishment of a principle of choice (according to whether one wishes to treat the documentation exhaustively, or adopt a sampling method as in statistics, or try to determine in advance which are the most representative elements); the definition of the level of analysis and of the relevant elements (in the material studied, one may extract numerical indications; references – explicit or not – to events, institutions, practices; the words used, with their grammatical rules and the semantic fields that they indicate, or again the formal structure of the propositions and the types of connection that unite them); [...] the delimitation of groups and sub-groups that articulate the material (regions, periods, unitary processes); the determination of relations that make it possible to characterize a group (these may be numerical or logical relations; functional, causal, or analogical relations; or it may be the relation of the "signifier" (*signifiant*) to the "signified" (*signifié*). (2004, 12)

Such variety and articulation at more levels enable history to bypass the usual questions about the rationality of historical flow and teleological projection, and to overcome its own field limits through inevitable intersections with disciplines like linguistics, mythology, economics, literary analysis.

Despite claims to the contrary, I would suggest that Foucault's approach shows traits belonging to structuralist analysis in that a particular site is defined on the basis of the relations it entertains with its vicinity; what is different, though, is the deliberately provisional, negotiable nature of both relations and limits arising from a plurality of voices, none of which is reduced to silence or mainstreamed, and the choice to avoid cultural totalities like "the spirit of an age" or definitions borrowed from anthropology.

The change is neither complete nor easy to accept as even the historians involved in it experience a resistance to open the very uncertain and potentially destabilizing territory of difference and dispersion. The security provided by a history constructed through recourse to the myth of linear origins, antecedents and traditions projected teleologically to justify the present is compromised by concepts like "separation", "threshold" or "independent system", which question the very idea of generalizing theories. Moreover, it is difficult to let go of a kind of collective reassurance derived from the uninterrupted flows that traditional Western history pursued by knitting past events into ideologically determined syntheses embracing man and accompanying him into the future, just as it is difficult to renounce the restitutive function thus performed that ensured that whatever had eluded man would be restored. It is "as if we were afraid to conceive of the *Other* in the time of our own thought" (2004, 13).

While acknowledging deconstruction theory's and postmodernism's exposure of the crisis of cultural authority in Western thought and questioning of Western epistemological codes, post-colonial scholars lay great emphasis on the particular circumstances their practices originate from and resist inclusion in the former's debate on Otherness and history as yet another universalist paradigm that would enclose them in the contradictions of the very system they are challenging, thereby subjecting them to a new form of colonialism. Therefore, building on the fictive nature of historical reconstruction, they have articulated more culture-specific analyses grounded in difference rather than essence and aimed at revealing the mechanisms at work in the production of colonial history as well as the system of organized knowledge in which it is inscribed. As Ashcroft *et al.* point out, post-colonial scholars endorse the postmodern fragmentation and cultural crisis of Western historical discourse as a starting point, but the wounds and trauma provoked in their societies by expropriation and the violation of rights demand a double engagement: thus, reading against the grain, they look for weaknesses and gaps in the master narrative, but are also committed to claiming their past by bringing to light hidden evidence and voicing silenced stories. Perhaps the most comprehensive enterprise in rewriting colonial and post-colonial history is the founding issue of the Subaltern Studies Group, namely the need for Indians to represent themselves in history. Reclaiming their own ancient tradition and contesting the status of sovereign theoretical subject conferred to Europe by academic historical discourse, whereby other countries' histories became "variations on a master narrative that could be called 'the history of Europe'" (Chakrabarty 1995, 383), Subaltern Studies aim to appropriate the "antihistorical devices of memory" and the "antihistorical 'histories' of the subaltern classes" (1995, 384), that is, of peasants and workers, as constructions of the past producing modes of self-representation. Criticism, however, has been expressed by Spivak and Chakrabarty, who question the procedure adopted on the ground that the inclusion of the mythological element typical of antihistorical narratives would be subjected to the rules of evidence and the linear sequence that the writing of history demands, so that the subaltern could only be spoken for and spoken of, without finding any real space to become part of the theoretical knowledge, as the tendency will always be that of reducing them to instances or quotations in the larger statements formulated by scholars. Chakrabarty calls for a yet to be written "provincialization" of that Europe made universal by imperialism and nationalisms not by simplistically rejecting modernity, liberal values, reason and so on, nor by resorting to an ever-deferring cultural relativism, but by investigating what allowed Enlightenment rationalism to become established and "obvious" well outside Europe, and by writing a history that

> deliberately makes visible, within the very structure of its narrative forms, its own repressive strategies and practices, the part it plays in collusion with the narratives of

citizenships in assimilating to the projects of the modern state all other possibilities of human solidarity. (1995, 388)

Refuting the idea of pure and disinterested knowledge, Edward Said envisaged all cultural practices as directly or indirectly linked to the operations of power: "The power to narrate, or to block other narratives from forming and emerging, is very important to culture and imperialism, and constitutes one of the main connections through them" (1993, xiii). In time, culture solidifies around the concept of nation and becomes a source of differential identity on the basis of which boundaries are defined and diachronic national or regional narratives are produced, further legitimizing its existence. At the basis of Said's position are Foucault's reflections on the role of discourse in the construction of power and Gramsci's conceptualization of hegemony which, although generated by concern for the working class in the wider frame of Marxist thought, has awakened great interest in post-colonial studies because of its distinction between actual political coercion and dominance obtained through ideas and culture, whereby education and cultural practices elicit the consent of the subordinate – hence the parallelism between a dual action that can be seen at work both in the institution and consolidation of the social order within a given society and in establishing and maintaining colonies abroad. According to Bart Moore-Gilbert, for all its brilliant insights, Said's *Orientalism* seems to evoke a rather atemporal vision of the Orient that does not include the movements that led to its creation; the reading of history upon which it is based ascribes power to the colonizers only, while the colonized would be further identified through the stereotype of the passive, sensual, feminine and mute Other. In *Culture and Imperialism,* instead, Said expands on the interrelations between the Western framework of knowledge and the non-metropolitan production and shows greater recognition of the resistance opposed to dominant power; at the same time, however, he also acknowledges the dangers involved in the turn to nationalism that this often entails, as the same essentialist divisions of colonialism are easily replicated.

Voicing the question "Of what is history made as it happens?" Gayatri Spivak (1999, 238) challenges the ways in which representations of so-called historical reality come into being by adopting a cultural analysis informed by "persistent critique" and favouring heterogeneity over uniforming visions of post-colonial cultures. Starting from the assumption that criticism must not reject the West, but rather negotiate with it, Spivak is willing to risk the uncertainty deriving from an approach deprived of any "totalizable analytic foothold" (Moore-Gilbert 1997, 79) in order to investigate how indigenous peoples were persuaded to substitute the version of reality provided by colonial history, cartography and ethnography for their own understanding of the world. Hence the attention on the one hand to the assumptions and the rhetoric of historical discourse and on the other hand to marginal lines of flight (e.g. minor figures and incidents) which are likely to reveal the bias of the historian's system of reference aiming to legitimize power. This is where attention turns to the "subaltern" and the "popular" as subjects and to their relationship as modes of enquiry into culture and history. This kind of oblique, guerrilla-like strategy is preferred to direct counter-hegemonic discourse as the latter runs a greater risk of being effaced or absorbed into binary logic, which would but reaffirm the authority of power itself. According to Spivak, redefining identity is perhaps the main area where subversive counter-hegemonic discourse can constructively engage with and integrate previous restrictively convenient definitions of self as innate or given: not essentialist conceptions of origin or belonging then, which would just reverse existing ethnocentrism, but a dynamic, multifaceted construction that takes into account the many biological, social and cultural interrelations by which the individual is shaped.

More inclined toward a psychoanalytic reading indebted to Freud, Lacan and Foucault, Homi Bhabha focuses on the anxieties emerging from the negotiations between colonizers and colonized. Taking as a starting point his interest in the cultural exchanges in the history of British rule in India, Bhabha sees the deployment of stereotypes and the silencing of pre-colonial history as evidence of the destabilizing fear of fragmentation generated in the colonizers by their contradictory attitude to the colonized, and finds between the lines of the enunciation of the colonial present "a splitting of the discourse of cultural governmentality at the moment of its enunciation of authority" (1994, 131). In this light, the apparatus made of military parades, flags and the ensuing textualization of history constitutes a fetish brought in to contain political anxiety and make sense of "colonial nonsense" (1994, 132). In its enforcement of surveillance, colonial authority unintentionally incites sabotage and refusal, whose destabilizing effect is amplified by the contradiction implicit in the colonial attempt to impose on the subjects regulations and lifestyles of the metropolis and yet emphasize the divide by fixing the boundaries of identity. A specular attitude is identified in Western history, whose fundamental entity, the nation, Bhabha interrogates in its certainty and settled nature, as its horizontal and temporal boundaries are stretched and disrupted by contingent shifts; hence the need to read between the borderlines of established traditions and narratives so as to reveal the heterogeneity of the subject, his/her shifting margins and the lessons to be learnt from "those peoples whose histories of marginality have been most profoundly enmeshed in the antinomies of law and order – the colonized and the women" (1994, 151-52), since those minority discourses hardly contribute to the homogeneity of culture as it is portrayed, nor celebrate "the monumentality of historicist memory [and] the sociological totality of society" (1994, 157). As the transcendental vision of history is increasingly refuted, the focus of historical analysis shifts to the uncertainty deriving from the multiple movements of historical time.

The main criticism levied by post-colonial scholars against the Western recording of history concerns its monologic narration proceeding from a unified, privileged point of view, one that focused on Europe and on a vision of events streaming along one flow of cause and effect. An instance of this attitude can be found in the way the history of colonized countries is often recorded in European texts as virtually beginning with the colonial encounter: what had been before and the tradition that transmitted it were ignored. Such rendering of the past has been challenged as a restricted view elevated to the status of national or universal significance and given the quality of documented objective evidence, while the whole sphere of "difference" – different countries, chronological and spatial systems, values – was measured against this enlightened unifying discourse, found lacking, and dismissed as primitive or degenerate. Conversely, as Homi Bhabha stated in "DissemiNation" (1994, 199), the re-found visibility of peoples at the margins shakes the monolithic, imagined nation and gives birth to "counternarrations" whose uncertainty and raggedness can disrupt dominant ideologies.

Among the rhetorical strategies recurring in colonial discourse, David Spurr has identified some which apply to historical recordings of the colonial encounter. "Appropriation" justifies European presence in other countries as the response to an appeal from the colonized, which could either manifest itself as chaos calling for the restoration of order, or as a natural abundance of resources awaiting the arrival of those "who are best able to exploit them" (1993, 31). "Negation" works by denying the existence of whatever is perceived as ambiguous: as neither the language nor experience provide an adequate framework of interpretation, the Other is inscribed as absence, emptiness, nothingness or death, so that history and place are cleared "for the expansion of colonial imagination and for the pursuit of desire" (1993, 93); as a result, a people deprived of its own history can be compressed into someone else's, while the impossibility to find its own image undermines the strength to engage in the creation of new institutions. "Affirmation", which is the other side of the coin, consists in the need for colonialism to "always reaffirm its value in the face of an engulfing nothingness" (1993, 109), thereby demonstrating an assumed moral superiority and a duty to elevate peoples whose lives were allegedly ruled by instincts.

The Western historical model is, according to Aruna Srivastava, "an act of remembering forward in Barthesian terms" (1991, 66), that is, an operation starting from the end result and linking it retrospectively to the event to which its cause can be traced, in a sequencing of events that quite obviously has no autonomous unfolding without the historian's ideology. An example of this and other textual/ideological strategies is provided by the accounts of how, in 1815, the British conquered the Kandyan Kingdom in Ceylon, the rich and fertile part of the island which had maintained its independence in spite of centuries of foreign domination under the Portuguese and the Dutch. A well-established British historical tradition (including Rev. James Condiner and Governor Frederick North) used to motivate the intervention as requested by a faction of the Kandyan people suffering under their cruel king, Sri Vickrama Rajasinghe, whereas Henry Marshall, a surgeon with the invading army comments:

> It appears not to have been at this time deemed expedient to promulgate the real object of the war, which was obviously to destroy the national existence of the Kandyan government altogether and to annex the country to the British crown. [...] There seems to be a great propensity in the Saxon race to seize or acquire the possessions of contiguous estates without much reference to consistency, justice or good faith.
>
> [...]
>
> Much is said in this proclamation of the barbarous or uncivilized character of the king, as if we were to constitute ourselves avengers or guardians of the globe, and make the infliction of punishment different from our own a pretext for

war and conquest. The desire to possess the country opened our eyes to the delinquencies of its ruler; and to justify aggression it was deemed expedient to assail not only his character, but also the character of the Malabar dynasty consisting of four sovereigns, each of whom had been freely elected by the chiefs and people. (1846, 148-149)

Annexation was first sought through diplomacy by formally acknowledging that same king later portrayed as a tyrant: the treaty proposed – and refused – creates a different scenario, one which reads almost naive:

Article III. – In order to secure the honour and safety of the Kandyan majesty and his successors, his Excellency the Governor of the British possessions in Ceylon shall send immediately into his majesty's territories a detachment of seven or eight hundred men, which force may thereafter be increased as occasion may require; and as the troops are to be employed for the purpose of securing the king on his throne, and defending him against all his enemies, foreign and domestic, his Kandyan majesty agrees to defray the expense of four hundred men, with a proportion of officers of the said force. (1846, 81)

The Kingdom was eventually obtained through a mixture of treachery (another king was crowned), textual manipulation (a Convention was approved in which the British agreed to govern according to the customary laws and institutions of the kingdom and to maintain the rights and powers of the feudal chiefs and the Buddhist clergy) and military intervention, naively – or conveniently – responding to the belligerent provocations of another pretender to the throne. The rhetoric of the opening lines of the Official Declaration of the Settlement of the Kandyan Provinces is striking:

Led by the invitation of the chiefs, and welcomed by the acclamations of the people, the forces of his Britannic Majesty have entered the Kandyan territory, and penetrated to the capital. Divine Providence has blessed their efforts with uniform and complete success. The ruler of the interior provinces has fallen into their hands, and the government remains at the disposal of his Majesty's representative. (1846, 159)

A detailed account follows of the atrocities perpetrated by the king and the ensuing "impossibility of establishing with such a man any civilized relations, either of peace or war", so that the basis is laid for the Convention of March 2, 1815, in which it was agreed

"1st. That the cruelties and oppressions of the Malabar ruler, in the arbitrary and unjust infliction of bodily tortures, and the pains of death, without trial, and sometimes without an accusation or the possibility of a crime, and in the general contempt and contravention of all civil rights, have become flagrant, enormous and intolerable;

"2nd. That *the Rajah Sri Wickreme Rajah Sinha,* by the habitual violation of the chief and most sacred duties of a sovereign, *has forfeited all claims to that title, or the powers annexed to the same, and is declared fallen and deposed* from the office of a king;

[...]

"4th. *The dominion of the Kandyan provinces is vested in the sovereign of the British empire,* and to be exercised through the Governors or Lieutenant Governors of Ceylon for the time being, and their accredited agents, saving to the Adikars, Dissaves, Mohottales, Coraals, Vidaans, and all other chief and subordinate native head men, *lawfully appointed by authority of the British government,* the rights, privileges, and powers of their respective offices, and to all classes of the people the safety of their persons and property, with their civil rights and immunities, according to the law, institutions, and customs established and in force amongst them.

[...]

"11th. *The royal dues and revenues of the Kandyan provinces are to be managed and collected for his Majesty's use and the support of the provincial establishment,* according to lawful custom, and under the direction and superintendence of the accredited agent or agents of the British government. (1846, 273-276, emphasis added)

Interestingly, Marshall comments, "The British government assumed the despotism of the fallen monarch; the people having no legal power to control the decrees of the governor more than they had to modify the orders of the king" (1846, 176). In 1818, following a rebellion, a proclamation was passed to bring the Kandyan provinces under martial law so as to exercise stricter control and reduce the privileges and powers of the local chiefs. The changes thus introduced, the roads linking the interior to the coast and the seizing of land to establish plantations terminated the isolation of the Kandyan region and involved the transformation of pre-colonial social institutions to satisfy the needs of industrializing Britain.

Besides showing how teleological thought can refashion causes and effects so as to legitimize actions, the events sketched stimulate further reflection on the close link between history and textuality: in fact, as K. M. de Silva (1981) points out, once incorporated into the standards of English constitutional law, the territory was liable to increasing degrees of domination as the above treaty was open to amendments by subsequent legislation.

The unit formed by geographical boundaries and historical record consolidates into the political community of the nation-state which, according to Chakrabarty, has been universalized as the most desirable form by the joint efforts of European imperialism and Third-World nationalism (1990, 384). A widely accepted theory by Benedict Anderson, instead, locates the origin of the nation-state in the interaction of Protestantism and print capitalism as the key factor in fixing a few languages in written form (thereby endowing them with wider circulation and higher status than the others, which remained confined to the role of dialects) and creating "unified fields of exchange and communication" (1983, 47) which contributed to the emergence of national consciousness. Romanticism's promotion of folk character, national language, national literature as means to awaken in the people a strong sense of rootedness and belonging was so successful that in contemporary history the nation has become the standard expression of political consciousness, and practically "superseded the preceding 'cultural systems' of religious community and dynastic realm" (Chatterjee 1995, 164) by depriving any other formation of recognition and international weight.

If the national identity of a people is still in the making, or is perceived as threatened or inadequate compared to others, then the rhetoric of the nation easily slips into nationalism. Given the need to invent a historical continuity for unprecedented ideological formations and legitimize provisional political entities, recurrent strategies have been identified, such as a selective forgetting of a hybrid past and the celebration (or invention) of ancient, monocultural and heroic traditions constructed on "authentic" ethnic identities; an emphasis on "national" traits by elaborating binary oppositions to refer to in categorizing the foreign(er); the projection on remote times of essentially modern "scientific" identity classifications; the adoption of symbols and iconographies to boost unity; in short, the creation of an "apparatus of cultural fictions" in which "imaginative literature plays a decisive role" (Brennan 1995, 173). Drawing on the models developed by Western nationalism in over 150 years, the former colonies – claims Partha Chatterjee – have been able to consciously impose cultural homogeneity through military and educational state action following the model of Russia, resort to populist celebrations, images and political organizations as in nineteenth-century Europe, or advocate the liberal enlightenment and critique of regimes that characterized America. Common features provide a strong drive toward the definition of an absolute national essence to be opposed to anything external, the shaping of a collective memory proud of the continuum of its traditions which are portrayed as resisting the contamination of otherness, an insistence on the notion of purity and the reproduction of the same Manichean thought that justified the binary categorizations applied by colonialism. These kinds of "national liberationist narratives" are supported by critics and writers like Benita Parry, Frantz Fanon and Ngugi wa Thiong'o, who advocate the need to construct a "politically conscious, unified Self, standing in unmitigated antagonism to the oppressor" (Parry 1987, 30), "bring into existence the history of the nation" (Fanon 1961, 51), and even reject the language of the colonizers in order to realize a total decolonization and reclaim the space and the voice necessary to write the muted and invisible colonized back into history (Ngugi wa Thiong'o 1986). The impatience thus revealed derives from the perception of much post-colonial theory as apolitical and compliant with Europe, but, however understandable in the light of the suffering endured, the sheer rejection of the experience of colonialism and its legacy would envisage an abstract identity, one that dates back to the pre-colonial era and does not take into account the inevitable changes that the superimposition of another cultural system has generated. The protracted subjection to and interaction with another people must have set into motion mechanisms of reaction, adaptation, absorption that have remained in contemporary post-colonial societies; therefore, after an initial appeal to a militant sense of the nation, it is these subtler and more pliant strategies (to which Bhabha's mimicry and parody pertain) that constitute real subversive resources in dealing with the Western Other, while great attention must be paid to those subplots within the newly constituted nations that risk being marginalized twice.

The issue is particularly important when the notion of "pure" identity is defined in terms of ethnicity; the mutually excluding traits adduced as constitutive of communities living side by side are bound to create friction at best, conflict more often, since each group projects the image of itself as exclusively entitled to previously shared territories and histories. As in biased mapping, a simultaneous operation of erasure and reinscription takes place, whereby past coexistence and intermixing is denied while ethnic purity is reinvented and glorified. Sri Lanka is a case in point, as the following discussion will illustrate.

2.1 History and the Construction of Identities in Sri Lanka

In contemporary Sri Lanka, torn apart by a civil war that lasted for almost thirty years (officially 1983-2009, but there had been previous confrontations), the legacy of the long and complex layering of colonial domination was compounded by the country's multiethnic composition. Colonized by the Portuguese between 1505 and 1658, by the Dutch from 1658 to 1796 and by the British from 1796 to 1948, the then Ceylon was divided into a number of kingdoms that were gradually incorporated into a single unit under the colonial administration. From a cultural point of view, a certain degree of hybridization followed the introduction of Roman Catholicism, of the Dutch Reformed Church (which granted the converts certain privileges) and of the pervading socio-political and economic system established by the British, but great impact on the composition of society came from the unions between local women and European men, resulting in a distinct ethnic group – the Burghers – cohabiting with the Sinhalese majority, the Tamils and the Moors. Relations between the Sinhalese and the Tamils had at times been tense in the course of history, but the divide was exacerbated by the policy of divide-and-rule implemented by the British. In fact, apart from the Burghers, who because of their European ancestry were deemed superior to the other ethnic groups and virtually monopolized the professions, lower administrative positions were given to the Tamils as more reliable and more fluent in English, while the Sinhalese earned a reputation for laziness and indolence that relegated them to the margins of productive society. In fairness to the latter group, it must be said, however, that perhaps because of the terms of the 1815 agreement, education in English was widespread in the densely Tamil-populated Jaffna peninsula (although mainly through American missionaries), whereas in the south it was available only to a restricted urban elite, thus excluding large segments of the Sinhalese population. The other lines of divide were traced by religion (generally speaking the Sinhalese are Buddhist, the Tamils Hindu, the Moors Muslim and the Burghers Christian, although distinctions are much more blurred), but also by caste, regional provenance, language and gender. The nationalist movements operating in the years around independence, which was granted in 1948, adopted the same binary oppositions to delimit the "true" and dominant identity; thus, in pursuing the primary goal of getting rid of the colonizers, a revival of Buddhism allowed the sweeping rejection of Christianity, missionaries, Western habits and British rule by virtue of a process of identity affirmation whereby "an ethnic group is impelled to display its unity through visible symbols and overt symbolic actions or through the reiteration of grandiose ethnic myths" (Obeysekere, quoted in Silva 2004b, 100). The two major ethnic groups started to build on their own self-awareness and to develop identity codes, so that, for example, rules were prescribed for the Sinhala Buddhist lay person, integrated by the appropriate standard of conduct for women, while the Tamils strengthened their own ideology by extolling their religion, culture and language. What had been a shared opposition to the religion and cultural practices of the Europeans broke under competing anxieties of self-assertiveness, but what converged was the feeling that missionary education had corrupted women, thus jeopardizing the purity of both races. Dress, manner and behaviour became indicators of ethnic belonging: thus, the Sinhala woman was expected to wear the Kandyan sari to distinguish herself from her Tamil neighbour, who would wear "an Indian sari, a nose ring and a *pottu* on her forehead" (2004b, 102).

The rhetoric deployed by both factions in this attempt to "gender" the nation has been studied by Neluka Silva (2004b), who points out how the motif of the motherland is explicitly represented in a poster designed by the Ministry for Women's Affairs in the late 1980s portraying a woman breastfeeding her baby while dreaming of a soldier, accompanied by the imperative "Give your life's blood to nourish our future soldiers". The assumption that makes the equation possible is the construction of a certain figure of woman as pure, that is, Sinhalese, Buddhist and compliant with the requirements of race loyalty. Besides implying the "authentic" Sinhalese woman's approval of the war, this exclusionary identity immediately posits women of mixed ancestry, non-Buddhist and westernized in education and behaviour as "Other", not belonging to the nation and therefore unfit to be made into symbols. Besides the relation it bears with the fairly common representation of the land as feminine, the inscription of the motherland on a woman's body was also used by the Tamil Tigers, who revitalized old legends to provide suitable images for posters idealizing mothers proud to send their sons to war and strongly projected the desirable model by publishing in *Women and Revolution: The Role of Women in Tamil Eelam National Liberation* a photo of a Palestinian woman carrying a gun and a baby (Silva 2004b, 97).

The symbolism of the fairly recent nation-state was also constructed by locating the core of Sinhalese authenticity in the Kandyan region. As said before, the Kandyan kingdom succeeded in keeping its relative autonomy under Portuguese and Dutch rule, and even the British finally achieved control over the area only about twenty years after their arrival. While a certain degree of intermixing both in terms of customs and unions had happened between the lowland population and the Europeans, the Kandyan Kingdom kept its traditions and its separate identity, which, as Nira Wickramasinghe (2004a) argues, allowed both colonial discourse to consider it with a sort of nostalgic and respectful admiration for things preserved in their original, pure form, and nationalist rhetoric, hunting for emblems of the future state, to appropriate the Kandyan heritage as truly representative of the essence of Sinhalaness. Besides the importance of dress, the consolidation of which as "traditional costume" was also aided by the British custom to classify people according to ethnic groups and to prescribe the clothing of the various grades of officials (again an instance of a constructed Orient whose members *had* to look Oriental), a very revealing example is provided by the interest condensed around the return of the Kandyan royal seat to Sri Lanka. According to various sources, the throne was a present given in 1692 by the Dutch governor Thomas van Rhee to the then Kandyan king Vimala Darma Suriya II. The throne, "made either in Colombo by Sinhalese workmen under Dutch supervision or in one of the Dutch settlements in India by southern Indian craftsmen" (Pearson 1929, quoted in Wickramasinghe 2004a, 74) was sent to England in 1818, after the British crushed the rebellion in the five provinces and finally incorporated the kingdom in the colonial administration. Kept for over a century at Windsor Castle, the throne was returned to Sri Lanka in 1934, where it stirred debate as to its role in representing the soon-to-be independent nation. In fact, even before its arrival, when the news about the return spread, the Secretary of State received a message from the Kandyan chiefs, who protested against the handing over of the throne to the people of Ceylon rather than to their own as legitimate owners. As Kandy was going to be both the seat of the official ceremony and the home of the throne, the British Governor expressed his firm objection to further recognize the Kandyans as a separate people. Accordingly, the throne arrived in Kandy, was exposed for some days in the King's Pavilion and then taken to the capital, Colombo, where its exhibition at the local museum had to be extended to satisfy visitors. However, a subsequent change in the plans, namely its storage in the Treasury Room in the capital instead of Kandy, reinstated the throne into the property of the state and the people, thus transferring its perceived symbolic value to the nation as a whole. But the nationalist agenda did more: in the 1934 exhibition, the throne was described as belonging to the last king of the Kandyan kingdom, that same Sri Wickrama Rajasinghe deposed through joint manoeuvre by the British and his internal enemies, whereas today it is attributed to the father of the king who received it as a gift. This convenient rewriting of history has presumably worked by removing the link with the last king of Kandy (who, besides being portrayed as inhuman by colonial historians, met a very inglorious end) and establishing a new one with Rajasingha II, the father of the intended receiver, who had the merit of leading Kandy to the peak of its power. A number of operations were thus performed in the whole passage from hybridity to authenticity: 1) the mixed origin of the object was pushed aside in favour of a symbolic epitomizing of Kandyan identity; 2) Kandyan culture was seen as separate from the rest of the island and elevated to the status of "authentic" in both colonialist and nationalist discourses because of its enduring resistance to invaders; 3) thus nobilitated, "Kandyanness" could be read at a domestic level as a synecdoche for Sinhalese identity as against Tamil identity and as a proud symbol of unified Ceylon to be opposed to foreigners. The logic behind this process highlights an ideological reinscription of the material by biased historians, who in this case did not apply a chronological cause-and-effect pattern, but rather what White terms "a paradigm of explanation" that retrospectively gave the argument "a specific shape, thrust and mode of articulation" (1990, 67).

To this day a homogeneous Sri Lankan identity is hardly definable given the multiplicity of peoples and the ethnic divisions that brought the Sinhalese and the largest minority, the Tamils, to war. The widespread notion of two separate peoples with, respectively, Aryan and Dravidian roots in the Indian subcontinent is now being contested by several scholars as an arbitrary imposition interrupting the flow of social interaction, while the concept of a "pure" culture is refuted on the grounds of the inevitable and constant reshaping that has been taking place everywhere for time immemorial:

> If there exists such an oddity as a "pure" culture, it was so far back in time, at the early dawn of *Homo sapiens*, that speculation about it is an exercise in pointlessness. Cultures have been hybrid since that primordial moment. (Guneratne 2004a, 21)

Arjun Guneratne questions the validity of defining race in Sri Lanka on the basis of the linguistic categories "Aryan" (from northern India) and "Dravidian" (from the south) as artificial and too volatile. He contends that the widespread notion of the population of Sri Lanka as made of initial Aryan colonizers followed by successive Dravidian invaders is based on an arbitrary division which collapses in the light of a common form of kinship that differentiates both ethnic groups from the cultures of Northern India. Guneratne's argument is that Sri Lankans originate from southern Indian people who, moving in continuous waves, "settled among, and [were] assimilated to the social groups on the island which had arrived earlier" (2004a, 25). Objecting to a classification invented by nineteenth-century European orientalists and sustained by contemporary nationalist interests, Guneratne contends that the different languages spoken are not synonymous with racial diversity, as "the ability to speak one or another language is not determined by one's genetic inheritance" (*ibid.*); on the contrary, the Dravidian kinship system shared by both ethnic groups points toward a common past. Despite a sort of gliding over Muslim presence and the problems raised by hints at "previous groups" inhabiting the island, or by terms like "historically" and "at some point in the process", which in their vagueness seem unable to break away from the myth of origins and apparently credit a sort of mainstream historical knowledge, Guneratne does provide interesting and valuable evidence to support his theory. A re-reading of the two ancient Sinhalese chronicles, the *Mahāvamsa* and the *Cūlavamsa*, paints a picture of far more complex relations than the clear-cut opposition between Sinhalese and Tamils: intermarriage, for example, dates back to the founding myth of the Sinhalese, prince Vijaya's arrival on the island, reported in the *Mahāvamsa*, where mention is made of the royalty's habit of marrying princesses from southern India (the criterion being not ethnolinguistic but belonging to the same kingly caste), while the Kandyan nobles' offer of the throne to a south Indian Tamil-speaking prince, or the praise of Tamil kings found in both the *Mahāvamsa* and *Cūlavamsa* suggests that political relationships were not defined along ethnic boundaries requesting that each group be ruled by one of its members, but by prowess and other standards of proper kingly behaviour, just as in pre-modern agrarian societies there was supposed to be more in common between rulers of different ethnic groups than between ruler and ruled, the main distinction being that of social class and the habits and expectations it involved. Such assumption is supported by studies hypothesizing that the term *sinhala* was used in the *Mahāvamsa* to denote the ruling dynasty, whose name refers to the mythologized offspring of a union between a princess and a lion (*sinha*) and expresses a connotation of power, and that only later it was extended to the kingdom and finally to the people.

A further argument to defuse the competing ideologies of nationalistic discourse on both sides is the shared way of organizing the universe of family and marriage. Anthropological studies have identified six kinship systems, two of which – the Aryan and the Dravidian, named once again by borrowing from historical linguistics – prevail in South Asia. In Sri Lanka both ethnic groups are characterized by the latter, which is a system of cross-cousin marriages. Thus, while according to the Aryan rule one must marry outside the family excluding anybody related by blood, Sri Lankan culture favours marriages between the children of parents' siblings of the opposite sex, a practice which is recorded in the *Mahāvamsa* and appears to have been the norm in the sixth century, when the chronicle was composed. In other words, the children of one's father's brother or one's mother's sister are placed in the same category as one's own siblings and defined through the same lexical items, while the children of one's father's sister or one's mother's brother belong to a different category and are eligible for marriage. The commonality of system is mirrored in the language in that Sinhalese terminology referring to these relations is very similar to Tamil and shows scant traces of Indo-Aryan influence. Since the appeal to linguistic difference as a distinguishing element between ethnic groups is relatively recent and since language is more prone to change than the vision of the world at the basis of the codification of family relationships, the "irregularity" represented by the Sinhalese community speaking an Indo-Aryan language but organizing familiar bonds according to a Dravidian system might well point towards a much more hybridized population than nationalist discourse posits.

Darini Rajasingham-Senanayake (2004a) suggests that the European colonizers played a major role in the invention of ethno-racial identity because hybridity disrupted the judgemental racial classification on the basis of which they governed the indigenous population. The census was used as a tool to make sense of human difference, but the categories showed a superimposition of European distinction markers like "race" and "nationality" on local ones like "caste", so that in 1871 the first demographic enumeration showed a degree of overlapping as "Sinhalese" and "Tamil" were entered as both race and nationality, while "Kandyan" became a nationality.[11]

---

[11] The classification proposed by the already quoted Henry Marshall divided the population of Ceylon into five classes: "the Singalese, the Hindoos, the Moors, the Vedahs and the Burghers", thus mixing ethnicity and religion (1982, 12-13).

Ten years later the races were reduced from twenty-four to seven through the application of the so-called Scientific Method (law of Identity: A is always A; non-contradiction: A cannot be B and non-B at the same time; and excluded middle term: A is either B or non-B)", which informed colonial racial science. Neither language had a direct equivalent for "race", and the closest Sinhala term adopted – *jathiya* – referred to linguistic, religious, caste and cultural aspects as well as to the concept of nation, so that under one label a much wider frame of reference converged which collapsed other differentiations and justified its use, to this day, in that latter sense. Identity assumed also a territorial connotation, which to colonial eyes motivated the geopolitical divisions between Sinhalese in the south, Tamils in the north and Kandyans on the central hills. The polarization of opposed identities in the post-independence war between the Sri Lankan government and the Liberation Tigers of Tamil Eelam fighting for the creation of an autonomous state in the northern region, posited as an age-long conflict between the two "races", conveniently erases the differences between low-country and up-country Sinhalese and the commonalities shared by low-country populations. But, above all, the equation "Tamils = secessionists" ignores the request for regional autonomy made in 1925 by that same Kandyan area later advertised as the essence of Sinhalaness.

As both opposing factions lay territorial claims, priority in occupation of the land is a crucial issue that prompts the search for or the resurrection of foundation myths. Anthropologist Sasanka Perera provides an instance of political attempts at constructing a new hero through the appropriation by both Sinhalese and Tamil nationalists of the relatively minor mythological king Ravana. One of the protagonists of the *Rāmāyana*, Ravana, who flew a legendary aircraft, abducted Rāma's wife, Sita, and kept her captive in Lanka till Rāma, with the help of Hanuman, the monkey general, invaded the country and freed his wife. In spite of his military enterprises, Ravana impersonated what could be defined as the villain of the situation and it was mainly his airborne vehicle that impressed him in the collective memory, which however never really celebrated him as a hero. In the 1940s and 1950s the Hela Movement tried to prove the existence of an ancient pure language of the Sinhalese (Hela) originated in Sri Lanka and later contaminated by Pāli, Sanskrit and Tamil influences. The need to nullify Tamil claims together with fluctuating sentiments toward India were at the basis of a wider project – in which the Ravana episode was inscribed – to portray Sri Lanka as peopled before the arrival of Vijaya, the Indian prince recognized as the mythical ancestor of the Sinhalese who reached the island allegedly on the day the Buddha attained Nirvana. Moreover, owing to the similarity in toponyms, Ravana's fabled capital, Lankapura, was hypothesized to be in Sri Lanka, presumably pre-dating Kashyapa's fortress on the rock of Sigiriya, but no evidence has ever been found nor references in the folk lore of the area. Similarly, on the Tamil side there has been an attempt to establish early presence in Sri Lanka by referring to the two Indian epics written before the sixth century B.C., the *Mahabārata* and the *Rāmayāna*, where mention is made of the Naga Kingdoms (supposedly founded in northern Sri Lanka by the Nagar, a Tamil people immigrated from the south of India) being conquered by "Ravana, the Tamil Yaksha king of Sri Lanka" (Ponnambalam, quoted in Perera 1999, 68). Both settlements, then, would posit the Tamils as the original occupiers of the island "long before 543 B.C., which the Pāli chronicles date as the earliest human habitation of Sri Lanka" (*ibid.*). Thus, an ancient legend has been plied to serve opposed nationalistic causes; as Perera notes, however, neither version has really gained popularity, especially among the Sinhalese, whose descent from an Aryan civilized prince still enjoys wide acceptance.

To justify the violence and even the ethnic cleansing each front has inflicted on the other, nationalist histories have effaced a past made of mixed settlements, intermarriage, bilingual and bi-cultural communities in many parts of the island, but nowhere is this more

2 The Making of History

evident than in the Northern and Eastern provinces, where former regional and administrative demarcations have been replaced by a partition line recognized as "the border"[12] in the media and in the people's consciousness. While it was a fact that the north and northeast were predominantly peopled by Tamils, with the Sinhalese majority spread over the rest of the country, it is undeniable that the two ethnic groups lived side by side in both regions for a long time, experiencing sporadic outbreaks of tension, but on the whole coexisting, speaking each other's language and celebrating common festivals, especially in villages. The line cutting across the island used to move with the alternate outcomes of the war,[13] hardening for a long period into a real military border, the Forward Defence Line, stretching from Mannar on the west coast, through Vavuniya in the centre, to Batticaloa on the east coast and separating the territory controlled by the government in the south from the LTTE's in the north. Not marked on tourist or general maps, the border used to soften in times of relative peace while becoming an actual militarily presided line preventing passage in both directions in moments of

---

12 Interestingly, the term "border" is the same used to refer to the line cutting across Ireland (a country with which Sri Lanka has been exchanging experiences for some time now given the similarities in their status of ex-colonies and in the civil wars tearing them apart) and separating the Republic from Northern Ireland. The lexical choice seems to confirm Vita Fortunati's suggestion that the almost synonymic pair border/frontier does in fact connote different perceptions of the parting line: while the former denotes a clear-cut divide, the latter "somehow also brings together, brings to light a no-man's land", a territorial slice that still allows negotiations and interactions between the two opposing parties, which is exactly what the most radical ideologists of nationalism want to erase. (Lecture delivered at the conference "Cultural Memory in Geographical Peripheral European Countries", Malta, 7-9 May 2004, www.lingue.unibo.it/acume).

13 A personal experience of the extension of the war zone occurred in 1997, when the tourist authority defined the whole eastern coast up to Kirinda, much further south than the usual limit, "no-go-area", and informed that the "official" line actually sealed off the eastern and northern provinces as the Sri Lankan army was engaged in a mission – later abandoned – to clear the main supply route to the northern capital of Jaffna.

crisis; at all times, however, it stood as a symbol for either faction's reclaim of territory, with its correlated renaming process,[14] celebrated or condemned in the media as it shifted in one or the other direction by even a few metres. The Vanni region – this is the general denomination of the area in question – was known to have, already in the reports of the previously quoted colonial officer J. P. Lewis, an amazing variety of languages, customs, religions and peoples, a situation confirmed by the accounts of the elderly collected by Rajasingham-Senanayake during her ethnographic work in the field between 1996 and 1998. During the war, the most recurrent expression applied to the area was "the villages on the border" and the patterns of hybrid coexistence were replaced by military and refugee camps, while forced displacement by armed groups, which affected over one million people, destroyed communities where ethnic and caste divisions had previously been counterbalanced by shared social practices and bilingualism, thus promoting a mutually exclusive essentialism. The Sri Lankan government has recently announced the dismantling of such camps and the subsequent resettling of the thousands of internally displaced Tamil civilians that during the final phases of the war were detained there to be screened for possible links with the rebels, but the problem remains of how to go back to areas often no longer inhabitable after the fighting.

Although none of the material just referred to belongs to fiction proper, many of these "historical constructions" rely on narrative strategies adopted in literature and mainly present unified cause-and-effect sequences which however do not really stand the test of a closer analysis. The very central term "identity", which underlies textual and warfare strategies, shows a fundamental ambiguity of use, denoting the two opposing conditions of "being identical in every detail;

---

14 A notorious case is the village known by the name of Manal Aru which was seized, after indiscriminate killings on both sides, by the Sri Lankan army and renamed Wely Oya in Sinhala (University Teachers for Human Rights, Jaffna, www.uthr.org.lk, and Rajasingham-Senanayake 2004a, 52).

absolute sameness" and "being [a] specified unique person or thing" (*New Shorter OED*). Virtually forgetting the former, it is the latter that is emphasized in times of conflict and strengthened by anchoring its elusiveness to a variously portrayed cultural heritage as in the examples given before, as well as to land and time. However, fluctuations do jeopardize the solidity of such constructs as especially these two last dimensions seem to be exposed to tensions that suspend univocal value. Thus, the land cannot be taken as an absolute indicator of difference as territorial boundaries are continuously created, shifted and erased, but above all, it becomes an immaterial entity when war is deterritorialized and brought somewhere else. Guerrilla actions carried out in the main cities on either side, far away from the war zone, break the myth of fighting to defend one's own territory and, in the case of suicide attacks, at the same time sublimate and destroy that very identity that is being affirmed. Deterritorialization acquired strategic value in the Tamil Tigers' request to negotiate peace outside Sri Lanka (which might well have originated from safety issues) and in the government's refusal to do so as that would have meant conferring international recognition and equal status to a nation-state that politically did not exist, even if a *de facto* divide had been there for years. That time is subject to convenient interpretations too is revealed by the ways it can be stretched, plied and compressed in an attempt to trace origins that would support identity claims, or in the way war events are given a beginning and an end in media reports and historical accounts, while it is virtually just discourse operations that allow to isolate ongoing flows of activity and their consequences, as is the case with the 1983 ethnic riots in Sri Lanka, which cannot be entirely circumscribed to that historical moment since they kept going on for years, albeit on a different scale. Like many of today's conflicts, the strife in Sri Lanka confirms Thomas Hobbes' envisioning of time as a component of war, by which is meant not only the time of the actual fighting, but also the length of time each front knows that the other is ready to fight; at an ethical level, instead, the Sri Lankan situation has invalidated Plato's conception of *stasis* – or civil war – as requesting some restraint, for it was fought against one's own cultural kind and not against "barbarians" coming from the outside. That is precisely where essentialized identities lead to.

3 Language and Translation

"In the beginning was the Word" seems to appropriately synthesize the assumption at the basis of the whole discussion so far, since language is the means that allows more specialized formations to come into existence, like the specific fields of cartography and history dealt with before. But language is undoubtedly a much more complex phenomenon whose development and ramifications multiply the perspectives from which it can be studied; therefore, while there is no pretension to an in-depth linguistic analysis here, aspects related to translation and to the use of language in the writing of post-colonial authors will be explored as conducive to a closer investigation of the texts chosen.

Language is a site of contention whenever cultures come into contact, be it in the peaceful yet deeply-felt desire to maintain separate identities, each with its correlated cultural heritage as in the case of wide supranational bodies like the European Union, in the preservation of minorities within larger and more powerful nation-states or in the aggressive context of colonization proper. Language is constitutive of identity, not so much in its definition of ethnic belonging (see Chapter 2.1), but rather in a way that reminds of the two Saussurean dimensions of *langue* (the system of conventions adopted by a community at a certain time) and *parole* (each instance of that *langue* in practice) because of the role it plays for the individual both at a personal and at a shared, collective level of experience. Seen in this light, language is one of the main elements in the formation of self because it is the instrument that allows experience to be translated into emotions to be expressed, knowledge to be organized and personality to be shaped through constant interaction with other members of the same linguistic community. It is also, at the same time, a link binding the community and defining it as against others, not just in a synchronic perspective, but also in its diachronic evolution, as it connects the present with the past and allows the articulation of memory as well as the transmission of heritage both for the individual and the group. Moreover, as highlighted by Foucault, language is power, a notion strengthened by the idea that control over the media means control over every aspect of the life of a society. Of the importance of rhetorical models, in fact, were convinced the Romans, who translated massively from and incorporated the Greek tradition, trying to model discourse on the most effective rhetorical tradition – identified in that of Attic orators – while naturalizing it in Latin to the extent that contexts were adapted to current circumstances and poets' names replaced. Further corroborating the relations between language and history, this instance of imperialistic translation is commented upon by Friedrich Nietzsche with reference to the (lack of) historical sense characterizing a given age, in this case the Roman Empire:

> How forcibly and at the same time how naively it took hold of everything good and lofty of Greek antiquity, which was more ancient! How they translated things into the Roman present! [...] being Romans, they saw it as an incentive for a Roman conquest. Indeed, translation was a form of conquest. (Robinson 1997, 62)

Also in more recent times colonizing countries laid great emphasis on language policies, while, conversely, resistance and decolonization movements focused on strategies of abrogation or appropriation of the European language introduced. Thus, the superimposition of English on existing language systems as the vehicle of communication between colonizers and colonized, of commerce, administration and education allowed and consolidated a much bigger imperial project, while for the indigenous populations it represented an effacing of their cultural experience and the donning of a new habit – or mask, to use

Fanon's term[15] – that would make them and their countries (imperfect) copies of the metropolitan centre.

After extolling the virtues of English language, literature and science, reminding how that language guarantees access to the "intellectual wealth, which all the wisest nations of the earth have created" and slighting Indian culture as a body of ridiculous fairy tales, Thomas Babington Macaulay's *Minute on Indian Education* (1835) reveals its real intent:

> We must at present do our best to form a class who may be interpreters between us and the millions whom we govern; a class of persons, Indian in blood and colour, but English in taste, in opinions, in morals, and in intellect. To that class we may leave it to refine the vernacular dialects of the country, to enrich those dialects with terms of science borrowed from the Western nomenclature, and to render them by degrees fit vehicles for conveying knowledge to the great mass of the population.[16] (quoted in Ashcroft, Griffiths and Tiffin 1995, 430)

The vertical transmission thus envisaged constitutes an instance of hegemonic discourse in Gramsci's terms, a way in which certain attitudes are imbibed in a social class or, as in this case, a people, to such a degree that even when the circumstances of the conditioning cease to exist, the attitude is kept and perpetuated as an almost inborn trait. The recognition of such inherent dynamics of power explains why the whole domain of language and translation has been identified as a powerful locus of resistance, carried out by post-colonial scholars and creative writers through a number of practices that Ashcroft,

---

15 Frantz Fanon, *Black Skin, White Masks*, trans. Richard Philcox (New York: Grove Press, 2008).

16 A much longer section of the Minute is included in *The Post-colonial Studies Reader,* eds. Bill Ashcroft, Gareth Griffiths, and Helen Tiffin (London: Routledge, 1995), 428-430.

Griffiths and Tiffin (1989) group under the labels of "abrogation", that is, a rejection of the stylistics and the rules of correct usage of the imperial language as well as the underlying idea that words can be transferred to a different reality and still retain their meaning, and "appropriation", that is, the bending of the imperial language so as to make it expressive of the local cultural experience. While the former is typical of the early phases of resistance, it is the latter which has been exercising a more subversive and therefore destabilizing effect on English, which owing to the many varieties developed all over the world is now frequently referred to as "english" or "englishes". The superimposition of English on other linguistic and cultural systems left gaps where specific areas of experience could not be covered and it is often in these gaps and in the tension between the two systems that difference is inscribed. Apart from the white settler colonies, which tend to be monoglossic, the other post-colonial societies mainly present situations of diglossia – with two languages currently used, as in South-East Asia and most of Africa – or polyglossia, as in the Caribbean, where the intersection of various dialects and languages results in a linguistic continuum. These cross-cultural environments have proved very fertile for linguistic innovation as authors, increasingly aware of the limitations inherent in the search for an essential cultural and linguistic purity, have been exploiting the subversive potential of hybridity. Thus, the effort to describe culture-specific experiences using English but rejecting its way of structuring the world with reference to class or race or time, for example, has brought to light a series of strategies that "abrogate the privileged centrality of 'English' by using language to signify difference while employing a sameness which allows it to be understood" (Ashcroft *et al.* 1989, 51). It is interesting to notice how close the most relevant features characterizing resistant and appropriative writing are to the domain of translation, as in both cases a relationship is created between two languages with their respective systems of meaning, usage, style, syntax, and the cultures they are an expression of.

3 Language and Translation 81

Perhaps the earliest marker of difference in post-colonial works is the insertion of words belonging to the indigenous culture, not in order to give some local colour, but to evoke the cultural distinctiveness of a certain reality which translated into English would not be equivalent. This might seem a truism given the fact that the concept of perfect equivalence is considered utopian by most translation scholars and translators, aware as they are that even the most basic lexical items of a language denote and connote objects that do not necessarily share the same characteristics in another,[17] but it is an authorial intrusion that brings into the text a feature symbolically standing for a silenced culture. Sometimes such "lexical otherness" can be glossed, either through a parenthetical translation or through a paraphrase explaining it:

> So Minnie had become a novice and when she visited us in her Audrey Hepburn *Nun's Story* outfit the servants called her – of all things – Minnie *mausi*. Little mother, they meant, but I couldn't help finding the sound of it a bit creepy. (Rushdie 1996, 211)

In his pursuit of irony, Rushdie's explanation has the double task of clarifying a totally opaque word and further highlighting the contrast between its intended use by the servants and the expectations the sound is likely to generate in native speakers of English; in this case the strategy is a more complex one because the culture-specific item is homophonous with the English "mousie/mousy" and quasi-homophonous with "mouse" which collocates with "Minnie" to identify a cartoon character. The label is further complicated by the fact that "Minnie", in turn, is homophonous with "mini", the prefix to

---

17 A noun like "bread", for example, has different referents when translated into, say, Italian, French, Arabic or Sinhalese and, while evoking different images in the minds of the speakers/listeners, it also carries different connotations of warmth, softness, family bonds or social values which inevitably will be hard or impossible to convey.

denote smallness, and it is also an altered childish version of "mother". The effect thus created is a displacement not just of the language, but also of the reader, who risks being lost in a series of intersecting allusions. More frequent in early post-colonial writing, glossing is now increasingly abandoned (if not in instances where, as above, the layers of signification multiply) owing to the recognition that the choice of an English label would reduce the complex aggregation of meaning to the referent and establish an equivalence which would make the marked stylistic choice redundant. Moreover, experiencing growing visibility and a greater willingness to open to other cultures on the readership's part, post-colonial writers incline toward the bolder strategy of leaving culture-specific words untranslated:

> The room was stored with the past. Senani's past. An old, dark *pettagama* with a broken leg, a rock horse with a broken saddle, an old desk piled with uncorrected school books. [...] After some hesitation I lifted the heavy lid of the *pettagama*, brushing aside the cobwebs. (Wijenaike 1994, 9)

The Western reader is actually at a loss meeting the first occurrence of *pettagama* although, because of its collocation with adjectives like "old" and "dark" and the proximity of "leg", speculations will be restricted to either the semantic field of animals (toys, given the context) or furniture. It is the second occurrence which solves the doubt, even if no precise description or English approximation is given, so that a somewhat disturbing uncertainty remains around the object. The flow of reading is thus interrupted and a more active engagement is demanded of the reader, who has to become a translator and work out the meaning from the network of references – fill the gap in a sense – and it is precisely that gap that is important in signalling non-total homologation and the refusal to bend to the superiority of the colonial language. Lexical items thus highlighted function as metonymic of difference in that they embody a minoritized language, but they are also perceived as controversial because the underlying view is one that postulates the immutability of the cultural essence inherent in each word, whereas the whole postcolonial idea of subverting and appropriating English is based on the possibility of displacing the language from its centre and re-placing it in the new context.

Ashcroft *et al.* identify a second strategy in "interlanguage", a term used in linguistics to refer to the provisional system developed by learners during the process of acquisition of a second language and characterized by regular patterns which, although deviant from standard or "correct" usage, show in the recurrence of certain mistakes the existence of internalized rules. Difference is manifested at the level of syntax, which reproduces local usage, but it is important to overcome the idea that variations equal mistakes, as this would deny the legitimacy of regional varieties of English now included in descriptive studies. Moreover, interlanguage seems to overlap with what Ashcroft *et al.* term "syntactic fusion", which they define through reference to "Gabriel Okara's attempt in *The Voice* to marry the syntax of his tribal language, Ijaw, to the lexical forms of English" (1989, 68). English words are used, but the resulting sentences do not correspond to standard structures; again, the reader has to decode messages which, though recognizable at the level of single surface units, produce an alienating effect as they are moulded on the deeper structure of the mother tongue. Thus, considering that the deviations learners' interlanguage shows are usually the result of L1 interference, it is difficult to trace a line between the two strategies, which seem to be better defined by Chantal Zabus' borrowing of the term "relexification" from Loreto Todd[18] as "the making of a new register of communication out of an alien lexicon" (1995, 314). Deliberately deployed, relexification does not aim at mimetic reproduction of actual speech, but rather at the constant suggestion of another,

---

18 Todd spoke of the "relexification of one's mother tongue, using English vocabulary but indigenous structures and rhythms" (Zabus 1995, 314).

unfamiliar, language beneath the surface, whose rhythms can be accommodated through modifications in syntax. The process, reminding of Bronislaw Malinovski's word-for-word translation into English of the answers he collected from a south Pacific tribe to show the mental structures governing their speech, is variously described by authors deploying it as a kind of internal passage from the mother tongue to English and vice versa, or as an initial kernel of a few lines in the mother tongue that are then translated and further developed in the target language. It must be pointed out, however, that it is not simply a matter of translating a full-fledged text from a native into a European language because that would keep the two systems apart without creating any cross-cultural space, which is the new dimension where contact takes place. The hybridity obtained through relexification is rather a way to negotiate the national and international vocation of post-colonial texts because the writer is able to speak both *to* his/her people by using a language which is closer to their usage and *for* them to a much wider readership through a bidirectional movement that at the same time nativizes English and internationalizes local aspects.

> "Von Bloss! Today studying you're going to do?"
> "Yes, sir."
> "Then books open. Homework you did?"
> "No, sir"
> "Why? Homework giving, must do."
> "Time hadn't, sir."
> (Muller 1995, 155)

The condition of diglossic communities is parodied in the example above, where a Sinhalese teacher addresses an English-speaking schoolboy, who in turn mocks him by imitating his syntax. Beneath the surface, the SOV structure of Sinhala is visible as well as a few other traits that will be better dealt with in section 3.1.

The coexistence of languages can also be rendered through code-mixing and code-switching, that is, the juxtaposition within the same speech exchange of words, phrases or full sentences belonging to two different linguistic systems, usually occurring when a sensitive topic is touched upon or a new speaker enters the conversation. While providing a means to hint at caste, class or gender, code-mixing and code-switching manifest yet another inscription of difference pointing at an underlying tension both in the text and the community.

In the "contact zones" (Pratt 1992, 6) created through colonialism, lasting exchanges have been happening between previously separate cultures whose practices of creation often mix writing and translation. Owing to the movements of populations between centre and periphery, a large part of the world has become a contact zone whose biggest current manifestation, as Sherry Simon (1999) argues, is the West. The fluidification of cultural values and the coexistence of vernaculars and vehicular languages of international communication that characterize today's communities have led to a situation where "translation has come to figure prominently in contemporary literature" (Simon 1999, 58), either as an "implicit mode of literary creation in post-colonial writing or as an explicit source of inspiration in 'border writing'" (1999, 59). Therefore, because of the plurality of languages and cultures post-colonial writers deal with, the problems they face are similar to those presented by translation, as their activity is closely related to that action of carrying across expressed by the etymological meaning of the latter term. As Maria Tymoczko states, both are types of intercultural writing and, although the post-colonial writer is not transposing a text, but a culture "which acts as a metatext" (1999, 21) to be rewritten about, the analogy with the translator is found in the extralinguistic range of cultural factors that must be conveyed across a linguistic/cultural divide in the passage from one language to another. To further increase the intersections between writing and translation, there are writers who deliberately posit themselves as translators: in the choice of their characters' expressions, many Indian writers strive "not to betray the Indian text and context by an easy assimilation into the linguistic and cultural matrices of British English" (Prasad 1999, 43), and a similar role of mediation is identified by Moradewun Adejunmobi in much African writing. Thus made overt, this quasi-translation is an "attempt to make the process of reading as difficult as that of writing" (Prasad 1999, 54), while its African counterpart fulfils the different task of "promot[ing] authenticity through reference to an earlier version of a truly African story" (Adejunmobi 1998, 166). In fact, this has become a sort of convention that facilitates acceptance thanks to the fact that, in spite of the European language used, the content is deemed to constitute proof of its Africanness; a double constraint, then, for writers who, according to Samia Mehrez, find themselves in an "in-between" position, caught between the westernized post-colonial inheritance and "the 'traditional' national cultures which shortsightedly deny their importance and consequently marginalize them" (1992, 121).

The growing interaction between these two fields has resulted in the so-called "cultural turn" in translation studies, heralded by Lefevere and Bassnett's contention that "neither the word, nor the text, but the culture becomes the operational 'unit' of translation" (1990, 8); it has also drawn attention to the analogies between translators' and writers' linguistic problems and to the investigation of the role of translation in the constitution of empire, as the connection between translation and imperial ambitions dates back to the late fifteenth century, when exploration and the establishment of the first European colonies prompted writers and poets to celebrate the successes of their kings and queens in explicit lines. Thus, Antonio Nebrija is reported to have dedicated his *Gramática de la lengua castellana* (1492) to Queen Isabella with the explanation that "language is the perfect instrument of empire" (Robinson 1997, 60), while in his *Essay on Translated Verse* (1684), Thomas Wentworth, Earl of Roscommon, celebrated empire and poetry:

By secret influence of indulgent skies,
Empire and poesy together rise.
(Robinson 1997, 61)

After age-long debates on issues of translatability, literal translation against sense translation or fidelity against fluency, the second half of the twentieth century saw a progressive widening of the scope of research with more and more disciplines approaching translation as part of their epistemology, while its elusive nature lent itself to various angles of analysis, all relevant and shedding light on a particular aspect, but none exhaustive. Until the 1960s there prevailed a scientific method focused on single lexical units or phrases aiming to establish a system of abstract linguistic equivalences between languages which would allow universal and automatic translation processes; as it was a normative approach fixing criteria valid independently of the kind of text and strongly centred on the microstructure of the source language, it provided a restrictive and mechanical view of translation which ignored the influence of context. The 70s were characterized by a movement in the pursuit of equivalence from language segments to whole texts as units of signification and consequently by greater attention to case studies: following Roman Jakobson's assumptions that every speech act involves translation, that operations of encoding and decoding are included in every communicative situation and that every text inevitably incorporates a reworking of already existing material, the opposition between original and translation began to be questioned. Jacques Derrida further deconstructed the concepts of originality and authorship by pointing out how the foreign text ascends to the status of "original" only when it is deemed worthy of translation, thus entering a relationship that canonizes it and, to say it with Walter Benjamin, allows its afterlife. The difference in authority between source and target texts is thus problematized since the former is posited as dependent on its "derivative" form, which does not validate fame, but rather creates it.

The last twenty-five years have witnessed a shift of perspective whereby translation studies have increasingly embraced J. W. Goethe's vision of the translator as a mediator involved in the fundamental task to facilitate that process of dialogue and dynamic exchange between cultures that constitutes *Weltliteratur*, so that each text is no longer considered in itself, but rather as part of a complex network of cultural relationships. Based on a descriptive approach, contemporary studies have highlighted the idea of manipulation inherent in translation, which according to André Lefevere is always a rewriting of the source text, and as such the bearer of its own value and ideology, especially when considered in the light of the whole cultural production of a given society. While traditional modes of investigation further develop "pure" linguistic issues related to problems like the translation of tropes, the composition of meaning, the arduous balance between literalness and inventiveness, less orthodox contributions have been coming from discourse analysis, reception theory and, more recently, sociology, post-colonial and gender studies, so that a conspicuous part of the recent literature on the subject emphasizes the provisional, in-progress, and composite nature of translation. Avoiding prescriptivism, the eclectic approach thus developed does not reject the tools provided by linguistics, but focuses on the complexities of social and cultural phenomena around the single work[19] and claims the dignity of originality for the

---

[19] While contributors from various fields have joined and hybridized the debate on translation, losing somewhat track of its practical dimension, a call for "a realist model of translation procedure" (Uwajeh 2002, 228) comes from performative translatology, which rejects the preoccupation with making the target text sensitive to the context of the source as that "is not the object of translation, but a means to that end" (*ibid.*), and advocates the recuperation of the task of the translator beyond the pursuit of contextual equivalence, which is considered only one of the desired effects.

translated text too. Translation has been inscribed among the practices that can produce political and social effects because it contributes to the formation of cultural constructions; therefore, partiality and engagement are not only recognized, but even advocated if translation is to participate in the cultural emancipation of subordinate groups. According to Lawrence Venuti, in fact,

> the renewed interest in translation came because it illuminated minor languages, literatures and cultures with the help of the theoretical and political discourses that were then circulating in diverse syntheses, principally marxism, psychoanalysis, feminism and poststructuralism. (1998, 141)

The recent interest in margins and in the peripheral as not fully representative of the values of the centre, but rather pointing out variables, has touched translation, which – itself a "minor" art performed by "invisible" craftsmen – has been likened to post-colonial studies because its scope is precisely that of negotiating the foreign (hence marginal), rewriting it and bringing it into the receptor culture. Drawing on Deleuze and Guattari's definition of minor literature,[20] Venuti identifies the shared trait of minority cultural products in a kind of collective voice, going so far as to say that just like texts in a minor literature express more than the author's personal meaning, minor translation strategies evoke "a linguistic community, an ethnicity, a gender, or sexuality" (1998, 137) and, by reproducing the indigenization of the colonial language, they succeed in projecting transnational identities. However interesting, such a perspective seems to revive the kind of thought that postmodernism and post-colonialism strive to deconstruct, since while it may be a fact that on the whole minority literatures are more concerned with political and social

---

[20] The features characterizing a "minor literature" are: "the deterritorialization of language, the connection of the individual to a political immediacy, and the collective assemblage of enunciation" (quoted in Venuti 1998, 136).

issues, such binary oppositions as major-individual/minor-collective summarize generalizations that not only are not always tenable, but also move away from the contemporary approach which tends to privilege the specificity of single cases. Moreover, while the destabilization of the major language achieved through "formal and thematic innovations that are encoded with ideologies" (Venuti 1998, 139) can bring innovation and enrichment, it is not clear where the foreignizing should end before the translation degenerates into questionable writing or brings the source text to signify something very different.

Venuti's problematization of the foreign seems to echo some of the central issues debated in the second half of the eighteenth century in Germany, where Johann Gottfried Herder, and later the Romantics, felt the need to enrich their national language and culture through contributions coming from other traditions. It was not a desire to shed one's own spirit and language in order to surrender to foreignness, but rather an awareness that translation would highlight the limits of one's language and provide the means to "enlarge" it. This sensitive dialectic and the vision of the translator as endowed with genius and creativity is further elaborated by Friedrich Schleiermacher in "On the Different Methods of Translating" (1813),[21] the essay that marked a turning point in the study of translation by inserting it in the wider field of language and hermeneutic studies. Schleiermacher ascribed to the "real translator" the quality of originality and the ability to act on the target language by bending it to the syntactic and lexical peculiarities of the source and clearly distinguished between a translation that "brings the author to the reader" and therefore domesticates the foreign, as against one, which he favoured, that "brings the reader to the author", thus allowing the linguistic and cultural difference to mould the translated text and requesting an interpretative effort of the reader. Despite the similarity of approach, it

---

[21] "Über die Verschiedenen Methoden des Übersetzens" (trans. Susan Bernofsky, 2004) was originally a lecture delivered at the Berlin Academy of Sciences.

must be pointed out that the German Romantics' programme started in circumstances identified by Itamar Even-Zohar (Neergard 1978) as conducive to intensified translation activity, namely the moment in which a culture is "young", "weak" or peripheral, when it faces a crucial turning point or when it is in a stasis: by translating foreign literature, a principle of innovation is activated, and new influences are introduced which may re-shape the receiving culture. In fact, in the light of the internal divisions of nineteenth-century Germany and the heavy consequences of the Thirty Years War, the openness to innovations from abroad suited the political agenda to revitalize the language and literature. In spite of its convenience for nationalistic purposes, Schleiermacher's programme is raised by Antoine Berman to an ethics of translation that makes the text a site where the cultural "other" is manifested, albeit in the terms of the target language. A foreignizing strategy would thus partly counterbalance the ethnocentric violence that translation contains in itself from the very moment a foreign text is judged and found meritable according to the values inscribed in the importing culture, also because those very inputs that are meant to enrich the receiving system can at the same time undermine it by challenging its canons and values, so that by opening to innovations, systems risk radical transformation. Therefore, even if the German scholars were appreciative of the accomplishments of other cultures and abhorred the *belles infidèles* of French Classicism, their aim was to elevate thought and acquire more articulate modes of expression as means to create a national tradition, thus using a method that confirms Anderson's theory about print capitalism as one of the driving forces for the emergence of nation states and nationalism. So proud were the Germans of their imports from foreign cultures that even Goethe, who was certainly sensitive to the subtleties of the *Sprachgefühl*, claimed that soon other nations would no longer need to learn foreign languages in order to read works in their original versions as the German translations brought out the real spirit.[22] The translation model that had prevailed in the preceding two centuries was dictated by France, recognized in Europe as the epitome of refinement and human progress and allowed free manipulation of the text – which could be shortened, extended, changed in tone, depurated of vulgarities – so as to suit the dominant taste. It was such assimilation that the Germans condemned, acknowledging instead the value of foreign contributions, but their attitude became also one of conquest[23] and hence similar to the metaphors of translation as fight and plunder used by St. Jerome and John Florio, among others.

Foreignizing or non-fluent strategies, then, defined as "a close adherence to the foreign text, a literalism that result[s] in the importation of foreign cultural forms and the development of heterogeneous dialects and discourses; [...] a translation method along lines which are excluded by dominant cultural values in the target language, [...] a historical interpretation of the foreign text that is opposed to prevailing critical opinion" (Baker 1998, 242-43), are not new *per se*, but new seem to be the reasons for their use, that is, the valorization of alterity as such and a willingness to see languages and cultures as open systems perpetually influencing one another. In this respect, however, pointing out the native-language impoverishment of Ireland, Michael Cronin warns against universalizing one particular translation practice and argues that a distinction must be made between major and minority languages: while for the former non-fluent, resistant strategies "can be seen as a bold act of cultural revolt and epistemological generosity" (1998, 147), the very survival of the latter may depend on more conservative, naturalizing techniques

---

[22] Johann Wolfgang von Goethe, *Schriften zur Literatur*, quoted in Berman 1992, 11-12.

[23] "So today we make peaceful raids into foreign countries, especially the south of Europe, and return laden with our poetic spoils" (August Wilhelm Schlegel, quoted in Robinson 1997, 59).

which will resist the pressure coming from major languages especially in the area of lexis, a danger particularly felt in the current technological globalization whose time-space compression has made all languages minor compared to English. Starting from a view of the relationship between translation and minority languages as either assimilation, whereby speakers self-translate themselves into a dominant language, or diversification, that is, a preservation and widening of the minor language by translating back the inputs coming from the major, Cronin challenges the current mistrust of individualized communities and almost forces the ideal of hybridity into a context that seems to advocate impermeable monocultures:

> The defence of the particular [...] can be derided as the last refuge of the essentialist, but it can be seen equally as the *sine qua non* of genuine hybridity. Indeed, it could be claimed that in this context, strong identities produce interesting differences. (1998, 148)

Ireland also provides material for Tymoczko's (2000) study of translation and engagement: in the light of the fact that the inherent partiality of translation makes it also a political act working both in support of the power practices of dominant cultures and as a tool of resistance for colonized people, a complacent attitude is manifested toward manipulation in translation in the name of ideology at the expense of an integral rendering of texts as works of art. Finding analogies with translations of the Bible of the fourteenth and fifteenth centuries – which were strongly conditioned by the need for (or the refusal of) a democratization of the text so as to make it directly accessible to ordinary people,[24] the conflict between Rome and other

---

[24] The notion of "direct access" is contradictory as, in spite of the linguistic, theological and historical importance of Martin Luther's translation of the Bible into German, an approach that assumes translation never to be innocent cannot but question his neutrality, as the very existence of a translator – and hence a mediator – exposes the fallacy of the idea.

theological centres, the perpetuation or the disruption of specific doctrinal aspects like the worship of saints – Tymoczko analyzes translation "as a sort of speech act" (2000, 26), whose illocutionary and perlocutionary strength impacts on society, mobilizing it and bringing about change. Responding to Douglas Robinson's criticism (1997) of the huge socio-political issues raised by post-colonial translation theory which make it difficult to avoid generalizations, Tymoczko suggests isolating particular translation movements in their geographical and historical context so as to overcome this limitation. Her reference to the Irish literary revival at the turn of the last century implicitly hints at the previously formulated idea of translation as the relocation of holy relics to a more secure place to facilitate the spread of a cult (Tymoczko 1999) and posits early Irish texts of various kinds translated into English as fundamental for the emergence of Irish nationalism and for firing up the country in its reclaiming of independence, a defeat that for the British Empire would prove much greater than the material loss of the island as it provided "paradigms of textuality and action that inspired the rest of the colonized world" (Tymoczko 2000, 28). In order to claim a history and a culture, as well as construct an identity independent of British images of Irishness, myths were revived and actually nobilitated to counter the humiliation of colonialism. Thus, Cú Chulainn lost his most roguish traits and became an uncompromising hero inspiring militant nationalism through interlingual and intersemiotic translations that saw him in books, theatre performances and murals, later appropriated by both Protestant and Catholic activists as a symbol for their relentless fight. While translation went hand in hand with liberation activism in Ireland, thus realizing the movement from subjugation to autonomy via dialectical opposition to the colonizer that constitutes the utopian narrative of post-colonial studies, Tymoczko points out its responsibility in fixing an image of Irish culture that kept repeating itself after independence and promoting the ethos of violence. It was

Thomas Kinsella's irreverent deconstructionist rendition of Cú Chulainn, turned grotesque and anti-heroic, that shook the hardened political image of Irish nationalism: once again, translation contributed to challenge the *status quo*.

On a much wider scale, translation is also studied as one of the discourse practices used to control, "educate" and shape colonized populations by putting into practice Althusser's principle of interpellation, that is, "the calling of a person into subjectivity/subjection" (Robinson 1997, 23), and thus providing them with an image that, however partial or distorted, was assimilated. Translations of works from the Middle East show, according to Richard Jacquemond (1992), the hegemonic culture's inclination to adopt strategies that underline the difficulty and strangeness of the dominated culture, so that Arabic texts were, and often still are, translated "too literally" (1992, 149) into French and loaded down with paratextual information that makes reading a specialist's task:

> Such a conception of translation reinforces the same representations Orientalism has created: it inscribes in the structure of language itself the image of a "complicated Orient", as de Gaulle said, irremediably strange and different. At the same time, it allows Orientalism to reassert its status as the indispensable and authorized mediator between Arabo-Islamic and Western cultures. (1992, 149)

Similarly, Tejaswini Niranjana contends that Indians, represented as "Hindoo" subjects of the East India Company, came to see themselves as portrayed by colonial discourse – childish, mystical, irrational. In fact, "European translations of Indian texts prepared for a Western audience provided the 'educated' Indian reader with a whole range of Orientalist images" (Niranjana 1992, 31), while through the example of the translation of Sanskrit laws into English by William Jones, Niranjana points out the assumption that Indians were unreliable and therefore a European translator was needed to correctly interpret their laws and reproduce them in a purified form, a device which also allowed the British to claim that indigenous laws were preserved under their administration of the country. Niranjana also points to the complicity of the humanism of Western translation in the colonial project, especially in the intercultural translation used by anthropologists and ethnographers who accounted for asymmetrical relations between cultures by equating difference with a previous developmental stage of humanity. The intersemiotic translations that collected various practices into single target texts contributed to envisaging other cultures as unable to organize their systems in texts that ethnographers would translate, thus positing them as the givers of coherence to a "prelogical self-understanding" (Robinson 1997, 43). Such British-induced subjectification needs in Niranjana's opinion to be redressed by re-translating indigenous texts in a way that will posit the subject as increasingly decolonized. To do so, literalism is advocated, irrespective of the possible hindrance at communication; as Robinson notes, however, it is not clear how this can become a tool of decolonization, and, I would add, the approach seems to be rather elitist and based on the essentialist assumption of a pre-colonial purity and goodness.

The multiplication of perspectives from various disciplines and the wider scope of analysis introduced recently provide illuminating contributions to an understanding of translation both in its internal and external relations. However, it must be pointed out that Robinson's doubts about their concrete results for the profession are not totally misplaced, as no really transitive "law" has been formulated. While the translator cannot but profit from a knowledge of extra-textual dimensions that enhance the expressive potential of a word or a text, as well as from an awareness of the attitude underlying a specific strategy and the fact that a certain text might be part of a mainstream flow of foreign works or conversely be an element of rupture opening a window onto a yet unexplored tradition, the large cross-pollination following the appropriation of translation in many fields raises criticism because of its mostly theoretical angle and its reliance on post-structuralism as its dominant tool of analysis; indeed the word "culture" seems to be informing contemporary approaches to translation to the degree of bordering on vagueness, while the only way it can be grasped is by restricting investigations to very specific contexts that can actually provide insights into single cases, moving, so to say, from translational to translatorial studies.

The overlapping notions of source-oriented against target-oriented, foreignizing versus domesticating hint at a circularity in approach that, however motivated by different reasons, does not seem to really break new ground; thus, while the pursuit of literalness deriving from the ancient biblical tradition which required to maintain even the number and the order of words as expressions of divine will was increasingly abandoned because of the resulting awkwardness in the target language, favouring instead a fluent, reader-friendly rendition, today a new fidelity is called for, one that does not subserviently follow the author out of awe of originality, but that is able to identify those elements that embody crucial confrontations and that therefore have to be critically assessed and inventively rendered so as to convey their value of otherness and rupture. Here is where Philip E. Lewis's notion of *traduction abusive* (1985) comes into play: having identified a key unit of signification, it is for the translator to be bold and "abuse" the language beyond lexical equivalence to reach a wider dimension that activates the echoes and connections intended and avoids the traps that surface equivalence sometimes sets. Although it was not proposed in a post-colonial context, *"Vers la traduction abusive"*,[25] translated as "The Measure of Translation Effects", is an example of a rendering that problematizes equivalence not only at the semantic level, where "abusive" in English "does not immediately pick up another connotation of the French cognate: false, deceptive, misleading"

---

[25] Paper presented by P. E. Lewis at the summer 1980 colloquium "Les Fins de l'Homme", Cerisy-la-Salle, France; further developed and translated into English, it was included in Graham 1985.

(Graham 1985, 33), but also on a contrastive one, where both linguistic systems are analyzed in the wider frame of discourse, with particular reference to their modes of enunciation and scope of application, so that the potential abuse in translation "goes beyond – fills in for – the original" (Graham 1985, 42).

If translation is a key concept for exploring otherness and exile, then the text will have to retain "an alienness which will not alienate but enlighten the reader" (Ewbank 2003, 16) and emerge out of a relationship between the two that takes into consideration the manifold contextual parameters of the specific post-colonial situation and its links with the former colonizing culture as well as with other contemporary cultures. Such a relationship should not be programmatically politicized and subversive, but represent a moment of growth, an extra-dimension conferred to the source text by a privileged deep reading and an informed, collaborative rewriting.

3.1 Writing in English in Sri Lanka

As other former colonies, Sri Lanka is characterized by a polyglossic situation where a number of different languages coexist, intertwining at times, but basically keeping separate according to ethnicity or sphere of life. In a country where about 74% of the population speak Sinhala as their first language, 18% Tamil, less than 1% English and smaller groups speak Sri Lankan Creole Malay, Indo-Portuguese and Veddah, where many can communicate in both Sinhala and Tamil and relevant numbers have various degrees of fluency in English, translation becomes an inevitable dimension of everyday life.

As pointed out before, language was and is a site of contention both in its resistance to a foreign system and as a marker of identity and power in domestic relationships among communities that pursue the different goals of separatism against national sovereignty. The difficulty in reconciling different positions is evident in Article No. 18 of the 1978 Sri Lankan constitution:

18. (1) The Official Language of Sri Lanka shall be Sinhala.
(2) Tamil shall also be an official language.
(3) English shall be the link language.

While both indigenous majority languages are declared "official", the postponement of Tamil – whose addition was long asked for and finally made through the thirteenth amendment in 1987 – actually subordinates it to Sinhala and reveals its nature of addendum, suggesting a ranking that seems to find confirmation in the apparently irrelevant detail of a different capitalization, whereby only when used with reference to Sinhala are the words "Official Language" capitalized, which contributes to the acknowledgement of a more elevated status. Moreover, labelling English as the "link" language suggests an attempt at neutrality through a term chosen to somehow grant the unavoidable without conferring authority. But the careful legal disentangling of the language issue and the attempt to enhance one without openly compromising the other requires further definition, which is given in Article 19:

19. The National Languages of Sri Lanka shall be Sinhala and Tamil.

Distinctions are then articulated with great precision, with plenty of cases detailing when and where one, the other, or both, or all languages are requested or admitted, thus significantly producing one of the longest sections of the constitution apart from legislature.

English, introduced in Sri Lanka when the country became a British colony in 1796, saw its status rapidly deteriorating after independence (1948) and suffered the heaviest blow with the passing of the Official Language Act of 1956, which decreed Sinhala to be the only official tongue, thus virtually relegating non-Sinhala speakers to the role of second-class citizens. Later on, the introduction of quotas and qualification exams in Sinhala dramatically restricted access to university education and working opportunities in the civil service for

Tamils, Burghers and Muslims, whose knowledge of Sinhala very often did not meet the prescribed threshold requirements. Because of its colonial implications, English was banned from education, although the upper classes were still sending their children to international schools or abroad. Though not recognized as an official language, English evolved somewhat from being viewed as "a colonial hangover that would soon vanish" (Wijesinha 1998, 1)[26] and came to be gradually reintroduced, also in consideration of its international use as *lingua franca*. Today it is used as a kind of supranational language when Sinhala and Tamil speakers do not know each other's language, when neutrality has to be maintained or in fields of education, like law, where constant reference to previous analogous cases regulated in English makes it a necessity. In this schizophrenic situation, the standard English – however difficult it is today to define a standard for it – introduced by the colonizers has undergone a number of changes following the contact with local languages and, as in other former colonies, has developed its own Sri Lankan variety, even generating more hybridized systems known as Sinenglish[27] (an English matrix with a higher frequency of Sinhala words and syntactic deviations) and Singirisi[28] (a Sinhala matrix with scattered English terms or phrases).

It must be pointed out, however, that the notion of "Sri Lankan English" is controversial. Descriptive studies by Thiru Kandiah (1981), Siromi Fernando (1989, 1990, 2003), Manique Gunesekera (2000) and Manuel Herat (2001), explore the characteristics of Sri Lankan English and its contexts of use and identify a number of recurrent features including culture-specific loanwords, the use of the

---

[26] The wording is a pun on Sri Lankan James Goonewardene's novel *The Tribal Hangover*.

[27] A description of Sinenglish is provided in Wimal Wickramasinghe, *Sinenglish: A De-hegemonized Variety of English in Sri Lanka* (Nugegoda, 2000).

[28] A description of Singirisi in provided in J. B. Disanayaka, *Understanding the Sinhalese* (Colombo: S. Godage & Bros., 1998).

present continuous instead of the simple present ("On the instructions of the Magistrate, the Doctor who happened to be holding a degree from Madras and the nursing staff were arrested", quoted in Gunesekera 2000, 42); the universal tag question "no?" ("We must put this in the paper, no?", quoted in Herat 2001); reduplication to express intensity or duration ("All these days, cooking, cooking, from morning till night", in Fernando 1990, 111), and a tendency to add prepositions to verbs which are usually followed by a direct object ("Mount Lavinia will confront *with* Science College in the play off match", in Gunesekera 2000, 43). However, the validity of these observations is often questioned by other scholars: E. A. Gamini Fonseka (2003), for example, contends that such evidence testifies to a mastery of English at the level of an interlanguage to be discouraged as it would foster social inequality. Endorsing a prescriptive approach to language, Fonseka advocates policies that will curb "indiscipline in the study and use of English in Sri Lanka" (2003, 7). Old-fashioned as it may seem, this position finds its justification in the contradiction embodied by the "proponents of the so-called Sri Lankan form of English" (*ibid.*), who themselves use an internationally recognized variety and send their offspring to study abroad or at least at the British Council, while the formal acknowledgement of "substandard" deviations in school curricula would be detrimental to common people's opportunities on the international job market and ultimately lead to a wider gap between the haves and the have-nots in terms of language.

The ambivalent position toward English derives of course on the one hand from the desire to master a language which is necessary at an international level and on the other hand from aversion to a medium that is tainted by colonialism and perceived as perpetuating the same prejudiced mindset that informed British behaviour.

> The white folks told them:
> God save the King;
> We have come to civilize you

> And to teach you how to read and write –
>
> – With the lapse of seven decades
> She could write no more.
> But she could still
> Recite the scriptures in Pāli
> And read the newspapers in Sinhala,
> She even knew enough Tamil,
> To argue with the merchants.
>
> Can you read English
> Asked the white man
> In a sweat-drenched coat.
> Lost, the old woman
> Simply smiled.
>
> I thought as much
> The white man groaned
> And told the census-taker:
> Another illiterate native.
> (Perera 1995, 38)

A similar attitude was later adopted by the native elite, who "by denying English language education to the majority of the populace [...] managed to continue enjoying the special privileges they had accumulated" (Perera 1995, 41). Even today, Perera contends, rural areas and small towns do not get adequate English teaching, which is mainly confined to the cities, with the result that many graduates take up jobs that do not require English and thus hugely reduce their chance of upward social mobility.

> One of the most common answers I receive from undergraduates when I ask why they do not apply for private sector employment is: "Kaduwa nethi nisa kepila yanawa." "Kaduwa", which literally means the sword, is Sinhala slang

for English. What the above response literally means is that because they do not have the sword, they get cut off. They do not get cut off by the sword they do not have, but by the sword others do have! (1995, 42)

"Proper" English then cuts across society and provides the elite with a weapon that allows them to keep the urban and economic spaces closed to less affluent classes. Or, if the latter manage to break through social boundaries, the "weapon" of language is used to reduce them to *godayas*, inferior beings lacking control over English, or to crack language-oriented jokes that ridicule the trespassers.

For instance the George E. de Silva jokes popular among the English educated classes in Sri Lanka up to about the 1950s were based on de Silva's alleged misuse of English. According to one joke, a proposal was presented in the Municipal Council of Kandy to build a public urinal. At this point de Silva is alleged to have stated: "Why only a urinal? Why not an arsenal as well?"

> De Silva, a Sinhala member from the Rada caste had breached the social space of two elite circles: that of the Kandyan aristocracy dominated by the Govigama caste and the community of lawyers [...] dominated by Dutch Burghers. (Perera 1995, 43)

As the language of law was – and to a great degree still is – English, de Silva must have had a fairly good knowledge of it seeing that he managed to join the profession under those circumstances, yet the weapon was used to cut a divide which othered him through language.

Redeploying Ngugi wa Thiong'o's title, Perera claims that the Sri Lankan mind is still being colonized today not only through the pressing influence of globalized markets and cultural neo-imperialism, but also through the much more belated didactic practices of many international schools which still avail themselves of British-centric material that does not refer to local reality,[29] but teaches for example "the weather patterns in England, Wales and Scotland" (1995, 44).

Against this social and cultural background writers using English as their creative means of expression inevitably find themselves in a marginal position in their country. As D. C. R. A. Goonetilleke (2005) contends, they did not and do not form a movement, nor were they prompted by a desire to initiate anything like the Irish Celtic revival promoted by W. B. Yeats; individual voices, they were hardly heeded till the late 1980s or early 1990s, when the international success obtained by expatriate Sri Lankan authors Michael Ondaatje, Romesh Gunesekera, Yasmine Gooneratne and Shyam Selvadurai, the opening of the State Literary Festival to English and Tamil works too and the institution of the Graetian Prize by Ondaatje suddenly drew attention to creative writing in English.

However, whereas for Sinhalese and Tamil writers the means of English is a choice, it is not for Carl Muller and Michael Ondaatje who, as Burghers, have it as their mother tongue. While this clears the ground from questions about their political motivation, it does not prevent a measure of distance and estrangement toward their works, especially in the case of Muller who, although living in Sri Lanka, is hardly considered representative of the country.

---

[29] Reporting a personal experience, Perera gives the example of a 5-year-old child who drew a house, a car and a man and pointed at them as "Farmer John, farmer John's house and farmer John's car". Questions arise about the way the child will link her image of farmers and farmers' houses (the one she sketched looked like a postcard English cottage) with actual farmers – more often farm-workers – in her country, and how this image, added to the countless others she will assimilate, will shape her mind. The example might have been more striking by contrasting the child's construction of a farmer with the suicide of 13 farmers in Sri Lanka's dry zone, as that would have pointed to and explained a potential blindness in the urban middle and upper classes, unable to take notice of the hardship of villagers. However, Perera's summing up of their reason for suicide as "they could not come to terms with their existential dilemmas" (1995, 44) sounds too vague to support the hypothesis that they were in desperate financial conditions and not at all like farmer John.

In spite of the different circumstances, the notion of translated people seems to apply to both Ondaatje and Muller as, to different extents, they have had to reshape the relationship between language and environment and, much like Eva Hoffman's autobiographical self in *Lost in Translation* (1989), needed to fill the interpersonal gaps that separate them from representatives of otherness. Ondaatje, having left Sri Lanka for Britain and then Canada, experienced familiarity with the language but estrangement in relation to the environment, since the same words denoted different realities, or new realities appeared for which no linguistic means was available. Migration becomes then a physical translation (in the closest etymological sense) that originates cognitive processes similar to those informing translation proper when, dealing with a source text, the translator grasps it, peruses it, and yet finds it still elusive: it is not his/her own, it has to be made sense of and carried across for it to also make sense in another – sought for – dimension. Thus, Ondaatje can be seen as translated into an entity which simultaneously combines sameness and difference, since although self, memory and language are not eradicated, they certainly undergo transformations in response to the new circumstances surrounding them. But translation also applies to Muller, for whom, even leaving aside the relationship between standard English and Sri Lankan English, daily interaction means frequent shifts between languages and coming to terms with fairly widespread social prejudice toward the Burghers because of their "otherness" and the privileges they enjoyed in colonial times. To push the analogy further, it is a process through which the self is negotiated in a way that is similar to a unit of meaning being defined in relation to the elements in its proximity and to the general economy of the context, without ever losing its intrinsic source.

The mixed feelings toward English in Sri Lanka are probably at the basis of a certain neglect of its literature, which, as Rajiva Wijesinha argues, in spite of the international recognition gained by some expatriate writers, does not find adequate support from libraries and publishing houses. In this light,

> perhaps the single most significant event [...] recently was the decision by Penguin India to publish the novels of Carl Muller. Certainly the work of Shyam Selvadurai and Yasmine Gooneratne, despite their having lived long years abroad, conveys a strongly Sri Lankan flavour, but it was the work of Muller that really gave weight, in what is still largely a post-colonial world, to Sri Lankan experience, written up in distinctively Sri Lankan English. (Wijesinha 1998, 3)

4 Writing Within/Without/About Sri Lanka

Having embraced a view of discourse as constitutive of reality and never innocent in its shaping of representation, my contention is that the three strands followed so far – cartography/exploration, history, translation – are intersecting formations coming into existence through language and at the same time partial contributors to the definition of identity, itself strictly connected to and influenced by language.

4.1 Michael Ondaatje: Without (and About) Sri Lanka

Discourses intertwine and yet reveal their biases and fragmentation in Michael Ondaatje's writing. Born in Sri Lanka, but educated in Britain and Canada, where he now resides, Ondaatje has frequently engaged with issues reaching across the postmodern and the postcolonial, questioning dominant discourses, suggesting different readings and non-linear reconstructions that in spite of their being written on the page and therefore virtually fixed, never really reach a conclusion but rather hint at the unending possibility of a work in progress, a new translation.

While the search for identity can be seen as an overarching theme spanning across his three works analyzed here, different emphasis is placed on the means, or discourses, through which identity is looked at: thus, preoccupations with cartography and language prevail in *The English Patient* (1992), interrogations of history (and its more or less hidden layers) and translation inform *Anil's Ghost* (2000), whereas spatial and personal history are the keys to access identity in the memoir *Running in the Family* (1983). Never really defining himself as a post-colonial writer, Ondaatje has deployed postmodern narrative strategies that by offering a limited point of view, fragmented experience, excessive and contradictory characterization defy the notion of a coherent whole and the possibility of stable knowledge, hence following a path "from the assumed homogeneity of identity [...] towards an endlessly proliferating heterogeneity, whereby identity is endlessly deferred and replaced by a scenario in which the 'character' or figure constantly differs from itself, denying the possession of and by a self, and preferring an engagement with Otherness" (Docherty 1996, 63). Such negotiation with otherness, the interrogation of dominant modes of cartographic and historical representation, as well as the reflection on colonialism and the ensuing displacement – psychological and/or physical – of the colonized, have been increasingly present in Ondaatje's writing and contribute to a shift of focus towards a post-colonial engagement that, while certainly non-militant, shows nevertheless a desire to problematize the past.

Although his can be considered an experience of partial translation, as the move to the Western world did not imply a life to be reinvented in a new language, Ondaatje is an example of the "translated men" Rushdie refers to when talking about writers of the Indian diaspora (1991, 18). In fact, even taking for granted that the controversial peculiarities of Sri Lankan English did not compromise Ondaatje's ability to communicate in the foreign environment, the need to ply one's language to refer to new landscapes and new contexts does generate a sense of displacement and estrangement. Drawing on the elements highlighted so far, his characters[30] show non-monolithic identities that are negotiated little by little through interaction with others and the world in a perennial process of self-definition that re-elaborates the past to provide ever-new starting points. Thus, Ladislaus de Almásy in *The English Patient*, Anil Tissera in *Anil's Ghost* and Ondaatje's fictional self in *Running in the Family* are introduced and yet denied consistence, so that the reader must be willing to juxtapose the various pieces and accept contradictions in narratives as well as uncertainties in gender-roles, that is, abandon the illusion of reassuring identification and experience displacement him/herself. While acknowledging the complexity, the richly woven

---

[30] Reference will hereafter be made only to the characters featuring in *The English Patient*, *Running in the Familiy* and *Anil's Ghost*. When the titles are required in parenthetical notes, they will appear as *EP*, *RF* and *AG* respectively.

intertextuality, and the plurality of themes in the novels, especially *The English Patient*, my reading will mainly follow the lines traced in the previous chapters, allowing itself to "meander" in Ondaatje's style where the intersection of references calls for a brief foray in another direction.

4.1.1 *The English Patient*: A Eulogy of Deferral

Revolving around four main damaged characters, *The English Patient* is set in Tuscany but shifts continuously, through a host of flashbacks, to the Egyptian-Libyan desert between 1939 and 1942, juxtaposing experiences of geographical exploration and personal relationships under the impending threat – and then actuality – of the Second World War.

4.1.1.1 "I didn't give them a right name."

"I didn't give them a right name" (*EP*, 250), is the explanation the mostly anonymous English patient gives for his capture by the British soldiers garrisoned in Egypt when he finally reached a town after walking for three days through the desert to find a vehicle and fetch his injured lover, Katharine Clifton, lying in the Cave of Swimmers. And suddenly the almost rhetorical question "What's in a name?" is evoked and exploded: the "wrong" name – wrong because "everyone with a foreign name who drifted into these small oasis towns was suspect" (251) – becomes a catalyst for tragedy as identity is denied or gets transmuted. Paradoxically, in a narrative that places great emphasis on names and yet denies them stability, it is the Hungarian explorer and cartographer (and hence name-giver) Ladislaus de Almásy who loses all identification in a fire: disfigured after a plane crash in the desert, lost among his own non-sequential memories and deprived of his name tag, which is probably worn by a member of the Arab tribe that saved him when he "fell burning into the desert" (5), Almásy's identity vanishes, and new, temporary ones – the German spy, the English patient, the despairing saint – are pinned onto him during his translations through different countries.

Kept in life by the Arab tribe who however uses him to gain knowledge about Western weapons collected in the desert, the burned man is then taken to a British base at Siwa and finally transported to Italy, where puzzled Allies try in vain to prove him German. Moving up Italy in 1945, the camp hospital is set up temporarily on the hills around Florence, in the Villa San Girolamo, where the Canadian nurse Hana, traumatized after the horrors she has been witness to, decides to stay and look after the supposed English patient, now close to death and heavily relying on morphine. It is both through Hana reading out to him and through his ramblings with Caravaggio – a Canadian-Italian thief who knew Hana's father back in Toronto and manages to trace her – and Kip – an Indian sapper defusing the mines left by the Germans – that the English patient regains access to his lost memories and reconstructs, although in a fragmented and at times contradictory way, his identity and the events that led to the plane crash. The most revealing piece of evidence to yield insights into the unknown man's past is his 1890 edition of *The Histories* by Herodotus, made into a scrapbook containing "maps, diary entries, writings in many languages, paragraphs cut out of other books" (*EP*, 96) – a collage of impressions, thoughts and experiences which at the same time provide fragments of the history of exploration and of the European war in North Africa, for history, paraphrasing Ondaatje, is "a communal book".

Placing an explorer/cartographer at the centre of the narrative provides Ondaatje with a means to fictionally interrogate the complex relationship between geography and empire-building, following in the path opened by Joseph Conrad's essay "Geography and Some Explorers" (1926) and situating his protagonist between the "geography militant" that Conrad identified in eighteenth- and nineteenth-century expeditions and conquests of foreign territories, and the "geography triumphant" which enjoyed the fruits of the search. While on the whole empire tended to be looked at as a historical product, the choice to thematize the contribution given by the intellectual domination of space is, according to Graham Huggan (1989), a strategy used in post-colonial writing to revision the history of European colonialism and overcome the traditional history of geography that traces the evolution of "ideas about space and environment [...] to their present scientific state"[31] and portrays individual discoveries isolated from their social context.

Taking the map as a site where history, politics, geography and passions converge, Ondaatje reveals pervading dynamics of power which touch everyone, whether they are aware or not. Thus, some members of the expedition are in connivance with the British intelligence (Bagnold, Geoffrey Clifton), while even Almásy's innocence and dedication unwillingly pave the way for military action, and later – innocence lost after the British soldiers' refusal to rescue Katharine – he deliberately commodifies maps bartering them with the Germans in exchange for a vehicle to reach the Cave of Swimmers. The "last mediaeval war" (*EP*, 69) thus marks a dramatic turning point which exposes the hypocrisies of the supposedly civilized world: in the general dehumanization (which is further highlighted by the contrast with a setting imbued with Italian Humanism) Almásy's disintegration becomes a symbol for trauma and the crumbling of certainties. Nothing and nobody is whole any more, nor can actions, personal traits and physical environments aspire to unambiguous unity. And maps, among the most powerful products of teleological order, reveal their partiality and limitedness:

> On the frontispiece of *Kim* was a map with a dotted line for the path the boy and the Holy One took. It showed just a portion of India – a darkly cross-hatched Afghanistan, and Kashmir in the lap of the mountains.

---

[31] Anne Godlewska and Neil Smith, eds., *Geography and Empire*, (Oxford: Blackwell, 1994), 2.

[Almásy] traces his black hand along the Numi River till it enters the sea at 23°30' latitude. He continues sliding his finger seven inches west, off the page, onto his chest; he touches his rib.

"Here. The Gilf Kebir, just north of the Tropic of Cancer. On the Egyptian-Lybian border." (*EP* 167)

Their obsessive recurrence sheds light on Almásy's perception of himself – "I am a man who can recognize an unnamed town by its skeletal shape on a map" (18), "I knew maps of the sea floor" (*ibid*.), "Give me a map and I'll build you a city" (145); on his perception of the world – "all I needed was the name of a small ridge, a local custom, a cell of this historical animal, and the map of the world would slide into place" (19), "he drew maps that go beyond their own boundaries" (22), and on his relationship to Kip, which overcomes the initial gulf between an alleged representative of the Empire and an Indian subject, developing instead almost filial characteristics, or rather shifting traits from the cartographer to the younger man, himself a mapmaker engaged in discovering the geography of bombs and therefore related to "a map of knots" (111) and "a map of responsibility" (195), sharing with Almásy the ability to survey the world, scan the periphery, deploy the "rogue gaze that could look at an object or page of information and realign it" (111).

If "he who draws the map 'articulates' [...] the available space" (Punter 2000, 39), the English patient's inability to recreate order on the one hand reverses the silencing of the historical and geographical traditions of the colonized assimilated into the imperial project and on the other suggests the collapse of a system whose weaknesses he was conscious of. While Almásy's love for exploration is evident, he questions its nature and that of Europe's enthusiasm for discovery, the zest for mapping and human progress in the light of the ensuing discourse generated by a male-dominated ethos ready to endorse racial theory, slavery and exploitation. Thus, the attempt to chart (and own) the desert is a sign of presumption:

> the desert could not be claimed or owned – it was a piece of cloth carried by winds, never held down by stones, and given a hundred shifting names long before Canterbury existed, long before battles and treaties quilted Europe and the East. (*EP*, 138-39)

Moreover, it shows ignorance of its unfixed nature and an attitude that through re-inscription deliberately erases the signs left by the ancient civilizations that moved against its background before. It is the cartographer himself who denies the truthfulness of the borders on the map, as well as the illusion of the white man that he is the first to "discover" realities that have existed since time immemorial and were already known to others.

Despite his love for names and the reassurance they provide – like the harmony that reigned in the "fully named world" (21) of his childhood, or the sensuousness of the beautiful (often female) names "one can slip into" (141) in the desert, the English patient is critical of the widespread vanity of naming objects and places after oneself or in honour of one's nation:

> Still, some wanted their mark there. [...] Fenelon-Barnes wanted the fossil trees he discovered to bear his name. [...] Then Bauchan outdid him, having a type of sand dune named after him. But I wanted to erase my name and the place I had come from. By the time war arrived, after ten years in the desert, it was easy for me to slip across borders, not to belong to anyone, to any nation. (139)

Which is exactly what happens, except that the border he crosses does not allow return.

The urge to inscribe one's own name and consequently to establish ownership is related to old age:

> when we are young we do not look into mirrors. It is when we are old, concerned with our name, our legend, what our lives will mean to the future. We become vain with the names we own, our claims to have been the first eyes, the strongest army, the cleverest merchant. It is when he is old that Narcissus wants a graven image of himself. (141-42)

The vain anxieties which accompany old age are easily read as pointing to the decadence of European empires eager to replicate themselves abroad by inventing the myth of discovery, followed by military control and finally economic exploitation. However, the desire to look at a younger copy of oneself is reversed by the striking painting *David with the Head of Goliath*, an instance of Ondaatje's layered intersemiotic intertextuality that through reference to Caravaggio's double self-portrait as a youth and in old age – the former defeating the latter and "judging age at the end of [his] outstretched hand" (116) – provides an image for the ambivalent relationship between the English patient and Kip, while metaphorically prefiguring the disturbing familiarity that will oppose young nations to the old imperial world after independence. As J. U. Jacobs (1997) suggests, the image can also be read as the dynamic of identification and rejection informing post-colonialism, especially the confrontation between the post-colonial text and the canon or, more specifically, Ondaatje's novel "scrutinizing its many intertexts" (Jacobs 1997, 107), to which it is linked not through a filial, but through an affiliative relation.

The fairly common convention of projecting the landscape onto a (typically female) bodyscape is approached in the text less explicitly: thus, not only Almásy, but also Hana and Kip overlay the two dimensions in a way that is visible but avoids the most obvious voyeuristic expressions found in much travel writing and contributes to that permeability of borders which is so insisted upon. Bodies become micro-landscapes when Hana "loves the hollow below the lowest rib, its cliff of skin" (*EP*, 5), when her liking for "flesh the colour of rivers and rocks" (103) is met by Kip's "brownness of a rock, the brownness of a muddy storm-fed river" (105), in Caravaggio's eyes, which are "clear as any river, unimpeachable as a landscape" (39), or when the English patient runs his fingers through her hair and feels it "cool within the valley of his fingers" (42). It is however in relation to the latter that the overlaying acquires more sensuous tones which probably partly draw on the eroticism of much geographical writing, but mainly underline the link between his addiction to the desert and the adulterous – and addictive – affair with Katharine, the wife of a newly arrived member of the expedition. Thus, carried by the Bedouins, he is "within the larger womb of the canyon" (19) and, working at his book (in French) "coming closer and closer to the text as if the desert were there somewhere on the page [...] simultaneously struggled with her nearby presence [...] unable to remove her body from the page" (235). Talking about his explorations, Almásy tells how once mapmakers used to name places with the names of lovers or after women seen bathing, so that "a man in the desert can slip into a name as if within a discovered well" (141); then, after a few lines, in one of the many implosions of time and geography, the image materializes of a woman in Cairo who "curves the white length of her body up from the bed and leans out of the window into a rainstorm to allow her nakedness to receive it" (*ibid.*). What might look like the chaotic fireworks of a deranged mind provides instead a clue to follow the associations produced by memory, feelings and sensuality, as well as a first piece of information about something that will appear only later in the narrative. But it is also a way to establish a ramified connection, which is one of the *leitmotivs*, between the desert that "had been an old sea" (22) and was now crossed by "dry riverbeds" (4), and water, which "is the exile [...] the ghost between your hands and your mouth" (19), the only thing celebrated in the desert. A pairing of elements that mirrors the lovers: Almásy, the "desert Englishman" (48), mainly connoted at the beginning of the relationship by aridity, aloneness and sexual fire, and Katharine, "a woman who misses moisture" (153), seen "happier in rain, in bathrooms steaming with liquid air" (170), caught in a complementary union that finds the symbolic images of its impossibility in their separate ends, his through fire, hers in the Cave of Swimmers.

Hybridization is possibly the dominant aspect of the text, which deconstructs borders and posits them as shifting, open to compenetrations that defy the well-defined categories and identities deriving from the Enlightenment and informing so much of Western thought till the late twentieth century. If "in the desert it is easy to lose a sense of demarcation" (18), also buildings in civilized Italy are no longer self-contained units, but spaces in-between, showing features that belong both to inside and outside, like the library with a hole in the wall adapting itself "to this wound, accepting the habits of weather, evening stars, the sound of birds" (11); like the "doors that opened into the landscape" (13), or "the room which is another garden" (3), a chiastic reflection of the garden that becomes Kip's bedroom, where he sleeps, significantly, "half in and half out of the tent" (76); or the villa San Girolamo – itself turned into a desert where lost Western tribes stop temporarily before moving on – showing "little demarcation between house and landscape, between damaged building and the burned and shelled remnants of the earth" (43), a place that, as the title of the second section announces, is "in near ruins", hosting people similarly open to invasion, defenceless, "shedding skins" (117). Even books, symbolically used by Hana to replace the missing steps of the stairs, become passageways through which she "would emerge [...] feeling she had been immersed in the lives of others" (12), always yielding an unfinished reading as completeness is denied and replaced by deficit (sections missing, gaps in the plot) or surplus (new inscriptions and extra pages added by

Almásy first and then by Hana), thus constantly calling for a renewed engagement with the text which is the attitude Ondaatje demands of the reader, "never fully in balance" (93).

Permeability also blurs the borders of gender, as in an attempt to break the pattern of male writing that characterized exploration. It seems important, then, in a novel where exploration is the pre-text from which stories will flow, to include movements that destabilize that aspect too. Thus, in one of the many instances of intertextuality, Hana becomes Kim guiding the old teacher at night, but certainly more significant is the inversion of roles in her relationship with Kip, who starts to feel her presence while he works at fuses and realizes "he would be pregnant with her" (114), while, laying beside him at night, she lets his long hair free and finds that "she holds an Indian goddess in her arms" (218).

The English patient is part of that desiring machine that

> with its unlimited appetite for territorial expansion, for 'endless growth and self-reproduction', for making connections and disjunctions, continuously forced disparate territories, histories and people to thrust together like foreign bodies in the night. (Young 1995, 98)

However, he unmasks its assumptions and criticizes absolutistic attitudes, opposing them with an ongoing process of relativization:

> The ends of the earth are never the points on a map that colonists push against, enlarging their sphere of influence. On one side servants and slaves and tides of power and correspondence with the Geographical Society. On the other the first step by a white man across a great river, the first sight (by a white eye) of a mountain that has been there forever. (*EP*, 141)

Heroic figures are downsized. Thus, the image of the romantic explorers is countered by the bureaucratic side to their mission, which converts them from eager researchers into clumsy civil servants who tiredly fulfil the task of reporting to the Geographical Society in London. Lectures are monotonous, modest and inhuman in their scanty reference to casualties, as well as oblivious of "all human and financial behaviour" (132), thus respecting the prescribed scientific style free from rhetorical embellishments required by the association's protocol. The Geographical Society and the military secret service, the other British public body featuring in the book, cooperate in their roles of guardians of the hegemony established, which cannot tolerate deviations from the norm. Thus, as the Society perpetuates a format based on certain rules and promotes an impersonal style focused on scientific facts, the Big-Brotheresque intelligence keeps an eye on the adulterous relationship because, as Caravaggio tells Almásy: "You had become the enemy not when you sided with Germany but when you began your affair with Katharine Clifton" (255). Such a startling revelation, coupled with the casual comment that adultery does not figure in the Society's minutes, can be read as an attempt to safeguard the cultural formation that most provides continuity to the nation – namely marriage and the legitimate production of children – by hindering that union with an "Other" that is contained in the Latin etymology of the term "adulterate". In other words, the system in power mistrusts those elements that could make it spurious through the admixture of other substances, that is, through hybridization. It is precisely in this respect that Ondaatje's text works hard at collapsing distinctions, confusing metropolitan and colonial identities, right and wrong, centre and periphery.

4.1.1.2 "Cul-de-sacs within the sweep of history"

History permeates *The English Patient* and is continuously evoked as a complementary aspect of cartography. However, in spite of the many references to the context of the Second World War, the focus is not on factual circumstances, but rather on a way of connecting past and present that provides an alternative notion of history to the one endorsed by civilized nations now disseminating destruction.

In the first chapter, before he starts piecing together memories, the English patient acknowledges the influence history exerts on people when assimilated not cerebrally but through the senses, experienced – one would be tempted to say in this specific instance – on one's own skin. Considering the strength of the bond between the English patient and Herodotus' *Histories*, the book that with him survived the plane crash and the fire, my suggestion is that *The English Patient* grew out of it as a kind of rhyzomatic narrative which, allowing itself to be entered at any point, reproduces in its texture the same principles enounced by Herodotus and symbolized by Almásy interspersing his book with other material. It is a twentieth-century supplement based on the principle of accumulation and going against the reductionist attitude implicit in a narrative that channels events according to a linear sequence, a tentative chronicle open to the possibility of having to accept ambiguities and unaccountability.

> "This history of mine," Herodotus says, "has from the beginning sought out the supplementary to the main argument." What you find in him are cul-de-sacs within the sweep of history – how people betray each other for the sake of nations, how people fall in love. (*EP*, 119)

Could this not be the foreword to *The English Patient*?

In Hayden White's terms (1990) history is no less a form of fiction than the novel is a form of historical representation, and myth – I would add – is the overlapping dimension between the two, accepting both truth and falsehood as valid. Ondaatje's stories, imbued with myth, issue from a landscape of chaos and in their motion can either become clearer or fade back into it. This approach to storytelling mirrors the way in which Herodotus is said to be collecting histories in the novel, that is, intent on "piecing together a mirage" (119), and thus provides the model for a historian that is curious of the world and ready to accept its diversity. Both "historians" are located within an age-long tradition of writing about the Other, whose perception is obtained – just like that of the self – not by superimposing categories but by becoming collectors who, borrowing Benjamin's definition, gather "fragments and scraps from the debris of the past" (quoted in Saklofske 2004, 1).

Almásy's first attempts at self-reconstruction define himself in relation to the Bedouins who saved him from the fire. It is important to underline that the apprehension of the Other does not happen through sight, which in the tradition of exploration was the primary instrument for domination, but through the other senses – tasting the saliva of the mouth that chews dates for him, smelling the men around, hearing them and feeling the touch of the merchant doctor healing his skin – a physical contact that mirrors the breathing in through which "history enters us" (*EP,* 18). More important, however, is the fact that it is a nomadic tribe, a personification of a mobile thought that "focus[es] on the process, the very path, the journey itself rather than a point that marks the end of the journey" (Hillger 1998, 23), and hence of an attitude that is ready to explore what happens in the course of the encounter with the world. It is also the philosophy traceable both in the English patient's disregard for origins and in his exploration practice as, wandering like a desert Odysseus, he is open to changes of direction and does not allow the perspective of the goal to distract him from his immediate surroundings. By allowing diversions in the trajectory, then, one can enter cul-de-sacs that maybe will never lead anywhere, but that are worth exploring as they integrate the experience of the main path. This is what Herodotus does when he "travel[s] from oasis to oasis, trading legends as if it is the exchange of seeds, consuming everything without suspicion" (*EP,* 118-19). It is a revealing simile, as the seeds suggest the further germination that each legend can start, propagated as it will be by the nomadic Herodotus, himself open to be even contaminated from within through the ingestion of the Other's food.

The thematization of nomadism is apparent in the character of Almásy prior to the plane crash, in the other characters in the villa, who, as Caravaggio says, "are where [they] shouldn't be" (122), and especially in Hana, sleeping in a hammock that she hangs every night in a different place "preferring to be nomadic in the house" (13). The emphasis on nomadism is a way to respond to the radical nationalism that leads to the catastrophe of the Second World War, when civilization fights "the last mediaeval war" (69) that opposes barbarians to barbarians, and Western wisdom finds no better way to terminate it than by dropping the atom bomb on Hiroshima and Nagasaki.

If this history is the product of nations, then better to erase them, better to become nationless in the desert as the English patient did, trying to unearth the "lost history" (135) of which only rumours remain. Better also to believe Herodotus' book "of supposed lies" than supposed truths that have come to be accepted as such only because, as Kip says, "you had the histories and printing presses" (283), thus echoing Anderson's thesis about the fundamental contribution of print capitalism to the creation of those imagined communities known as nations.

The choice of a guidebook which posits history as plural from the very title, a book transformed into a collage that reveals a continuous, living interaction with its reader/historian and the possibility of constant re-negotiation through Derridean *différence* and *différance,* is reflected in the narrative itself, displaying three different arrangements of the memories of Almásy and Katharine's relationship, or looking at the war not from above (movements of armies, charismatic leaders), but from below, from the point of view of those who experience trauma and damage. Hence Hana's suggestion that every general should try the nurses' job, smell and taste death, before commanding attacks, or the contradiction between the extreme fetishization of nations as cultural and territorial apparatuses and a deterritorialized conflict fought outside their borders often using extraterritorial subjects. The alternative writing of history, then, is based on a humbler attitude that avoids a teleological reordering of events, acknowledges the existence of different accounts and various sources (as Herodotus, trying to define the Scythians, retells the rumours about them and confesses the gaps in his knowledge) and is ready to investigate them even when they might prove inconvenient,[32] thus rejecting an identitarian logic that sets up fixed categories in favour of a dialogical relationship with the Other.

4.1.1.3 "Words, Caravaggio. They have a power."

Difficult as it is to follow themes separately in this "labyrinthine" narrative (Barbour, quoted in Hilger 2004), I will now focus on aspects of translation and language, which inevitably will intersect the issue of names touched upon in 4.1.1.1. However, while names were looked at in the context of the practices of cartography, here the reference is more to the net of signification they create within the text.

The Villa San Girolamo, progressively taking in the four characters, features as a kind of "contact zone" in Pratt's terms (1992), where relationships and identities have to be negotiated as a consequence of cohabitation. It is however the name of the villa that provides a key to understanding the process that takes place there, as it

---

[32] Totosy de Zepetnek (1999) observes how although Ondaatje's was not a biography of Count Ladislaus de Almásy, the release of the homonymous film provoked an attack in *The Globe and Mail* of Dec. 4, 1996 that called the work amoral and ahistorical because it minimized the consequences of Almásy's actions and recast him as a passionate hero. In a letter published in the same paper on Dec. 6, 1996, Ondaatje answered:
> *The English Patient* came out [...] as a novel and the film version is not a documentary. [...] The facts are still murky and uncertain – to some historians he was a spy, some others think he was a double agent. [...] *The English Patient* is not a history lesson but an interpretation of human emotions – love, desire, betrayals in war and betrayals in peace – in a historical time.

is no coincidence that San Girolamo (St Jerome) is the patron saint of translators, himself known as the first translator of the Bible into Latin. And, in a continuing chain of associations, it is no exaggeration to say that the Bible – or at least biblical iconography – provides one of the most important systems of reference within the text, introduced from the very first page with the nurse washing the English patient and seeing in his burnt body the "hipbones of Christ", and immediately after with the narrator's comment that the patient is "her despairing saint" (*EP*, 3). Without engaging in a detailed analysis of biblical references, which would be beyond my purpose here, it is however interesting to notice that there are a number of semantically related terms that support this instance of less direct intertextuality. Thus, the Arab tribe rescues the English patient who is then "anointed" (6), placed onto "an altar of hammock" (*ibid.*), and "carried in a palanquin" (9) that prefigures the statue of the Virgin Mary seen by Kip at Gabicce Marine Festival; the shaman that heals the English patient's burns reminds him of an archangel and is later referred to as "this baptist" (10); the English patient is called by Hana "a saint. […] A despairing saint" (45), and he himself sees in Kip "one of those warrior saints" (109), thus providing an example of that transitivity of attributes between the man without a name and the "anonymous member of another race" (196), whose ultimate but unfulfilled passage is the English patient's offer of his "holy book" (294) containing, among others, quotes from Isaiah and Jeremiah and Solomon, to the sapper, who by now, after the atom bomb has been dropped, has severed all connections to the white people in the house. There are echoes of the Pentecostal gift of languages in Caravaggio's memory of a much younger Hana stepping onto a packed table at somebody's birthday party and singing in tentative French "*Alonson fon*" – sounds still disconnected from their signs – "miraculous with this new language" (53), while her skirt almost touches the flame of a candle and her ankles look "firewhite" (*ibid.*). And finally, the statue that holds Kip's lamp is St. Christopher, a man who in life used to help travellers cross a wide river in Lycia and a saint invoked for help in catastrophes. The etymology of Christopher as "Christ's carrier" makes his presence significant because of the link with the literal meaning of translation, as well as his patronage of pilgrims, travellers and – I would add – nomads.

That translation and the awareness of the power of words are crucial in *The English Patient* is pointed out in many ways, and certainly the striking collocations in which the verb "translate" is conjugated suggest on the one hand a retrieval of its etymological meaning of "carrying across, transferring", and on the other hand a stretching, an explosion of meaning that once again takes nomadic forms and explores untravelled roads. Thus, besides the relevant yet unmarked reference to Poliziano, who "translated Homer" (57), one finds marked choices in "[the English patient] was there to translate the guns" (20), "the buried switches that translated [the wires] from positive to negative" (101), "he translates the smell, evolving it backwards to what had been burned" (124), "[Katharine] was a woman who translated her face when she put on makeup" (248), and in many other cases that could lead the reader to hypothesize that the verb "translate" is used as a joker to replace precisely those "European words you can never translate properly into another language" (170). Plausible as this idea might be in a narrative that constantly reflects and refracts itself, the extreme attention devoted to words rather suggests that the pervading presence of translation is meant to convey something else – movement in space and time or, as Beverley Curran says, "deferment, for a translation is never definitive" (2004, 1). And deferred is, for example, the nurse's identity, an anonymous "she" for thirty pages till Caravaggio arrives to fill the gap about her preceding life, translating her into Hana from Toronto. Transition and temporariness – as well as a metonymic instance of the way translation was used to interpellate subjects (in Althusser's sense, see Chapter 3) – is made evident through the Indian sapper's name laughingly transformed into Kip by his fellow soldiers in England. An officer's reproachful "What's this? Kipper grease?" (*EP,* 87) at the sight of a stain on his report triggers a process whereby, without even knowing what a kipper was, "the young Sikh had been [...] translated into a salty English fish. Within a week his real name, Kirpal Singh, had been forgotten." (*ibid.*). Highly appreciative of all things English, Kip comes to like his nickname, but the horror at the news of the atom bomb and the sudden awakening to his brother's mistrust of the English prompt him to bundle the whole West under the same label: "American, French, I don't care. When you start bombing the brown races of the world you're an Englishman.[...] You all learned it from the English." (286), and from that moment he starts translating himself back into his older self, Kirpal Singh, wearing a *kurta*, weapons and rucksack now left behind.

The concern with translation in the novel is not with "meaning brought home captive" (Steiner 1975, 298), for in the war raging all around captives are too many already, and such a view would endorse the kind of appropriative translation that informed much colonial practice. What seems to be more at stake is an idea of meaning that progressively takes shape with every (additional) translation, just like the English patient's identity, the unfolding of his story and the lives of the other characters are continuously added to from different sources. Also, in keeping with post-colonial translation theory, such a mode problematizes authorship (the text is tellingly defined as "apocryphal") and legitimates interferences coming from translators/readers, as the alterations made to Herodotus' book confirm.

The "translational turn" in *The English Patient* authorizes a reading that sees in the protagonist a translator in many ways: a polyglot, an intersemiotic translator of the system of nature into linguistic and mapping systems, a mediator between cultures, well aware of the fact that language – a marker of identity – in his case dangerously multiplies identities, never really allowing him to settle in one. This translator pulls his listener/reader into his version by adopting a foreignizing strategy that bends language and refuses compliance with canonical narrative strategies as well as conformity to the "voices of abstract order" (*EP*, 285). Himself translated and displaced through cross-cultural experience, the English patient is an incomplete unit of signification. Drawing on the contention that "he has become a signifier without a signified" (Hilger 2004, 3), I would rather suggest that after the plane crash he has become a referent deprived of both a signifier and a signified: an object (a body) exists and is visible, but the word to denote it (a name) is not available, nor the mental image of it (his past life or any information about him). Striving toward unity requires a communal effort, which never fully succeeds since ambiguous pockets remain along the way, but slowly, as the name Almásy appears in the text, arousing Caravaggio's suspicion, it becomes more and more likely that the floating label will attach itself to the English patient.

The only character who evades translation is Caravaggio. He remembers a friend telling him that "words are tricky things" (*EP*, 37) and, as his mutilated hands prove, does not allow them to emerge easily. This paucity, which the English patient tries to overcome by reminding him of the power of words and asking him to speak – "You must talk to me, Caravaggio. Or am I just a book?" (253) – is what sets him apart from the other men in the house, allowing him to putatively replace Hana's father, in turn described as an ineffective speaker, somebody in whose sentences "you lost two or three crucial words" (90).

Katharine, too, is well aware of the power of words: in them she finds clarity and reason and through them she seduces Almásy, who is drawn to the voice that recites poetry and reads the story of Candaules and Gyges. But the overall enchanting effect of words is actually staged in a kind of transgendered *Arabian Nights* by the English patient, who keeps deferring death by narrating, literally suspending the sentence after his life has been woven a little further, thereby giving translation the character of transgression.

4.1.2 *Running in the Family*: A Piecemeal Sketch of a Family, a Country, an Era through Journeys and Rumours

A mapping of ancestry through memories and places, *Running in the Family* is defined in Ondaatje's acknowledgements as "a composite of two return journeys to Sri Lanka, in 1978 and 1980" (1982, 205).

"Incomplete," according to Ondaatje, the book is introduced by a map, two quotations (one on the fabled island of ancient times and one, satirical, on the consequences for Sinhalese and Tamils of not knowing English well enough), a fairly long table of contents and an atmospheric page where an anonymous "he" wakes up in the light and the imminent heat of a tropical dawn, twenty-five years after leaving his native country. A disquieting dream of his father surrounded by dogs in a tropical landscape opens the narration, making the I-narrator restless and impatient to set off from Canada, where he lives, and return to Sri Lanka, on a quest for knowledge about his father, his family, himself. The resulting *bricolage* of fictional passages, conversations with relatives and family friends, gossip, photos, poems, reflections on the country, words addressed to his father, provide dynamic, mythologized and comedic glimpses of a family but also of the last thoughtless years of the Burgher upper class.

***

In a paper presented at the Midwest Modern Language Association, Paul Jay (2003) basically agrees with some critics' contention that *Running in the Family* has an atemporal quality:

> *Running in the Family* doesn't seem to include the memory of colonization, and the exploration of personal identity largely ignores the long historical role British colonization

played in the formation of colonial and post-colonial identities in Sri Lanka. (2003, 1)[33]

Despite the further concession that "the book does engage colonialism in some important, if fleeting ways" (*ibid.*), Jay seems to find fault with both Ondaatje's lack of explicit condemnation of colonialism and his indebtedness to European culture, claiming that "for all intents and purposes, Ondaatje's is a Western autobiography, not a post-colonial one" (*ibid.*). A distinction such as this sounds forced, for, while it is a fact that (auto)biography as a genre belongs to the Western tradition, it will always revolve around the people, stories and places that have contributed to the formation of the chosen subject, so that adding the qualifier "post-colonial" just strengthens binary oppositions, for what would its post-colonial status be determined by? By the perspective assumed in dealing with the contents, by the contents themselves or by the physical provenance of the author? Obvious as this objection may be, I believe that a text described by its author as "not a history but a portrait or 'gesture'" (*RF,* 206) and explicitly dealing with the reconstruction of family history will *also* touch upon colonial and post-colonial issues (if applicable), but only with reference to the main theme, which is exactly what happens here. Although no direct connections are drawn between family events and the colonial (and, later on, post-independence) system surrounding them, the reader does find meditations about empire and echoes of its influence on people's life: they are conveyed in a fairly straightforward way where maps are dealt with, whereas history is actually less visible, almost smuggled in, and has to be gleaned among the bits and pieces of the narrative.

Places follow one another, as the protagonist visits and re-experiences them in the process of reconstructing his family's past and

---

[33] "Memory, Identity and Empire in Michael Ondaatje's *Running in the Family*", Midwest Modern Language Association, November 2003. http://home.comcast.net/~jay.paul/ondaatje.htm.

his own identity. What might seem a travel book, however, reveals its unconventional character through the protagonist scurrying here and there, following the prompt of each successive piece of information, but never really rationalizing a route.

The protagonist's need to go back and peel off the layers deposited by time and life experiences on his own self as well as on others in order to re-find a shared starting point has a symbolical counterpart in the geographical entity of Sri Lanka, whose important role in the narrator's process of re-tracing himself is underlined by the presence of a map at the opening of the book and by the attention devoted to the country's relationship to foreigners, whereby the island and the people in the book might be read as metonymically evoking each other. "I had already planned the journey back. During quiet afternoons I spread maps onto the floor and searched out possible routes to Ceylon" (22).

It is also a journey back in time: instead of simply buying a ticket, like an explorer the narrator looks for "possible routes" to Ceylon, one of the island's old names, availing himself of many maps since, given their unreliability, he may be able to gain a better perspective by collating them. The search for his family is colouring itself with romance, the protagonist a (mock) mythological or chivalric hero engaged in metaphorically and actually reading the book of the world on a quest for truth, however disguised, partial and fragmented it may be.

Cartography and exploration (and their consequences) are thematized in the chapter titled "Tabula Asiae", which opens with a series of "false maps" (63) portraying Ceylon/Sri Lanka in various epochs. In equating the maps to "translations – by Ptolemy, Mercator, François Valentyn" (*ibid.*), the narrator adopts a post-structuralist stance that by stressing their textual dimension elicits what Linda Hutcheon defines as a "suspicious" reading (1985). Besides, what is implicitly conveyed is the very modern – or actually postmodern – image of the cartographer as an intersemiotic translator, decoding a three-dimensional natural system and encoding it into a two-dimensional conventional system on the page, and a view of translation that through the emphasis on difference denies the ideal of transparent reproducibility of the source. But maps also depict the island as an ever-changing shape, at first as formless and primitive as an "amoeba, then stout rectangle, and then the island as we know it now, a pendant off the ear of India" (*RF*, 63). What this sequence hints at is the gravitational shift that happened in time, whereby the island that used to be seen from or in relation to Europe, is now defined by proximity to India – close to it, and yet detached – in an image that well suits the controversial relation between the two countries.

Around the maps, the iconography that often went along with mapmaking, with its display of animals and characters – a cherub, "ferocious slipper-footed elephants", "a white queen offering a necklace to natives who carry tusks and a conch" (*ibid.*) – constitutes a kind of orientalist inventory of projections derived from what cartographers fabled about, further reinforced by the dominant logic that informed European attitudes toward indigenous peoples. Because of their approximation and the reliance on reports from merchants and travellers, such maps reveal "rumours of topography" (*RF,* 64) but, above all, they expose "the routes for invasion and trade" (*ibid.*), thus evocatively exposing, in little more than one line, the core relationship between exploration, commercial interest and empire. Similarly, while the initial tone of the paragraph suggests that the Portuguese, the Dutch and the English could not but surrender to the soft sensuality of an island that "seduced all of Europe" (*ibid.*) – an image that seems to rely on the *topoi* of feminization of new lands and the alleged beckoning to the Europeans – a much cruder ending contradicts the elegiac tone by revealing that "invaders stepped ashore and claimed everything with the power of their sword or bible or language" (*ibid.*). The island/seductress becoming "the wife of many marriages" and having her name changed accordingly is read by Neluka Silva (1999) as one of the metaphors Ondaatje uses in the text (the other being the theatre) to establish his ancestry and the circumstances that contributed to the formation of today's Sri Lanka:

> The description of Ceylon as "the wife of many marriages" is more than an oblique reference to the egregious effects of colonialism and, like the marital relationship, foregrounds an antagonistic element. Similarly, in the light of this relationship between marriage and colonialism, the undermining effects of adultery and duplicity within the marriages in the text symbolise moments of pre-Independence resistance. The description of Lalla's position after the death of her husband, as liberated but '(managing) to persuade all those she met into chaos', may be read as a metaphoric enactment of the tensions of the post-Independence nation, carrying also a prophetic note of the state of affairs in 1983,[34] soon after the publication of the text in 1982. (1999, 2)[35]

It is interesting to notice that, while portraying Ceylon's history as a trail of subsequent colonizers who in turn imposed their own rule and world-view, thus adding a layer to a stratification that could only return a distorted image of themselves, the closeness between the various marriages and the island's transformation into a mirror which "pretended to reflect each European power till newer ships arrived and spilled their nationalities" (*RF*, 64) can be read as a sort of revenge the

---

34 July 1983 marked the worst outbreak of ethnic riots. After thirteen Sinhalese soldiers were killed in Jaffna by the Liberation Tigers of Tamil Eelam, wild mobs attacked the Tamils in the urban areas with the highest concentration (Colombo, Kandy and Trincomalee) devastating and setting fire to their houses and killing hundreds people. It took almost one week for the police to intervene and stop the criminals who, later investigations demonstrated, came from forces close to the then government.

35 Neluka Silva's article "Debunking ethnic labels" appeared in *Frontline* 16, no. 4, Feb. 13-26, 1999. Online edition http://www.frontlineonnet.com.

island took on the invaders, pleasing them superficially but ready to change with the newcomers as its only strategy for survival. This is an instance of transgression in Bhabha's terms that, coupled with the "parody of the ruling language" (*ibid.*) Ondaatje hears in his own name (a Dutch spelling an ancestor was rewarded with), raises the issue of mimicry as hybridized defence, producing episodes of civil disobedience within the framework of complacent civility.

In keeping with the tenor of the book, official history is hardly present; however, deploying his notion of the communal, Ondaatje mixes the personal and the public and drops almost casual hints at historical circumstances to be deduced from the events the family has to face, thus showing an approach that draws on Roland Barthes' questioning of the distinctions between fictive and historical narrative. Hutcheon finds that in Ondaatje's writing the narrator is a performer showing the reader the process of research and ordering of his narrative material, thereby creating what she defines "bio- or historio*graphical meta*fiction" through which "we experience that postmodernist performance in the act of reading the fragmented text" (1985, 304). Bearing in mind that the absence of a familiar model of narrativization is itself a narrative choice functional to the material, the next step would be to ask what has prompted it. And similarly, if the stories are set in Ceylon, and the narrator bothers to go back there, why is the island then so eclipsed? Why does it figure in glimpses but hardly ever in full view? While it is probably only for the author himself to answer, the hypothesis may be advanced that trauma impinges on the narrator, both on a personal level because of his parents' divorce and the subsequent migration to England and Canada, and on a collective level, not only as a kind of mnemic trace of being heir to a colonized tradition surfacing in the confrontation with the Western world, but also in the wake of the marginalization the Burgher community experienced in their own country, which led to massive migration to Australia and elsewhere. If that were the case, such a controversial relationship would actually be better dealt with if allowed to emerge sporadically, evoked by other characters, thereby reducing personal involvement to a minimum. In this sense, as Hutcheon says, "history [...] becomes a process, not a product" (1985, 306), and Ondaatje, aware as he proves to be of the subjectivity any form of writing the past implies, remarks:

> No story is ever told just once. Whether a memory or funny hideous scandal, we will return to it an hour later and retell the story with additions and this time a few judgements thrown in. In this way history is organized. (*RF*, 26)

Considering then his contention that "truth disappears with history and gossip tells us in the end nothing of personal relationships" (53), one could assume that history might well reveal something personal, whereas gossip might conversely provide illuminations on history. Which is what happens reading *Running in the Family*. For example, if in just two pages (25-26), while the narration follows its course, one also takes in the apparently marginal details around the characters, one hears "rumours" about the Dutch colonial presence in eighteenth-century Ceylon and learns that there are racial problems in modern-day Jaffna; later on, history surfaces through the graffiti on the rock face of the fortress of Sigiriya, "the first folk poems of the country" (84), followed by those written by the students held prisoner and tortured on Vidyalankara university campus during the insurgency of 1971. Similarly, the British empire is hinted at through the character of the paternal grandfather, Bampa, who "had a weakness for pretending to be English" (56) and lived in "his empire – acres of chosen land in the heart of Kegalle" (*ibid.*), which however by the close of the chapter has disappeared along with, it may be presumed, the end of the colonial era, as suggested by the clause "whatever 'empire' my grandfather had fought for" (60). But rumours of empire also seep through recurring references to British governors, to the high-ranking British officers travelling on the train the narrator's father hijacked, who upon discovery that "officers in the Ceylon Light

Infantry were going berserk and upsetting schedules [...] might just leave the country in disgust" (154), or through the description of the society gathering at Nuwara Eliya during the hot season:

> There was a large social gap between this circle and the Europeans and English who were never part of the Ceylonese community. The English were seen as transient, snobs and racists, and were quite separate from those who had intermarried and who lived here permanently. (41)

But while echoes of the "bigger" history are heard throughout the text, with the Second World War getting closer as the Japanese threaten to attack Ceylon, a "minor" history takes shape, namely that of the Burgher community, whose *dolce vita* starts to ebb in the 1930s to dramatically finish in 1948, when the country achieved independence. Although the lazy, thoughtless life depicted here characterized only the upper layer of the Burghers, the community's general inclination toward Western values and lifestyles and the privileged status enjoyed in colonial times kept them rather separate from the rest of the population, in a kind of buffer in-betweenness that lost all comfort in the nationalist developments that heralded, and then followed, independence. In Monica Turci's words, "a 'realistic' discourse based solely on facts could not [...] have illustrated the surreal condition of the Burghers" (1999, 248), who actually figure in fairly surreal tones also in Carl Muller's "factionalized" stories, where "the backdrop is fact, the centre stage fiction, sometimes exchanged, transposed" (1995a, xiii). In *Running in the Family*, political and economic insecurities become more and more visible as members of the family lose their jobs, as the money starts to be tight and women like Lalla and her friend Rene, "after years of excessive high living" (115) have to work in their dairies to make ends meet, while the biblical flood in which Lalla dies a spectacularly great death symbolically announces the end of an era and the beginning of a new order metonymically embodied by the Sinhalese family taking possession of the Kegalle estate. As the Sri Lankan playwright Ernest MacIntyre remarks, although "life was quite harshly real for most subject races of the British Empire" (1985, 315), there were niches of "comfortable unreality creeping into the lives of the upper classes of the subject peoples" (*ibid.*), that is, Sinhalese and Tamil gentlemen who studied in England and ran their estates or worked in the Ceylon Civil Service, and the Burghers. But while the former were able to adjust to the changes brought about by independence and rely on a system based on race, caste and politics, the latter "were to enjoy an entire mortality of heightened unreality, a surreality, because they wouldn't be provided with even a humbug of 'a tryst with destiny'[36] at midnight in 1947" (*ibid.*). Sensing the changes in favour of the Sinhalese looming in the Donoughmore Constitution of 1931, the Tamil minority grew more determined to safeguard their rights, while the Burghers "staged a complete retreat not only from the political life but also from other sectors of life. This was carried to the extent of leaving the island for greener pasture" (Peacock 1989, quoted in Turci 1999, 253). This growing disillusionment is mirrored in the last part of *Running in the Family*, where disgregation has happened, family members and friends have migrated to other countries, and the isolated and drunk figure of the father remains to epitomize the consequences of such retreat and loss of identity – silent, still and invaded by "branches that put their arms into the windows" (*RF*, 189), a symbolic image of the local overpowering the alien.

4.1.3 *Anil's Ghost*: The Ordeals of Identity

Ondaatje's first novel set in Sri Lanka, *Anil's Ghost* (2000), deals with ethnic and government violence in the country several decades after independence from Britain. It opens with forensic pathologist Anil Tissera returning to her native island after fifteen years in England and the USA, on a UN mission for human rights finally

---

36 MacIntyre is playing with the phrase used by Jawaharlal Nehru in his speech "On the Granting of Indian Independence" on August 14, 1947.

allowed in after pressure from Amnesty International and other civil rights groups. With the government-appointed archaeologist Sarath Diyasena, Anil tries to literally unearth a hidden piece of truth after some contemporary bone findings from a sixth-century location raise the suspicion that the state-controlled archaeological site is being used to bury recent victims of political violence. If identified, the skeleton would speak for the thousands who between the early 70s and the late 90s disappeared in the huge waves of abduction, torture and murder unleashed on the population by opposing factions. With the help of the epigraphist Palipana and the craftsman Ananda, the identification is completed, but, not fully trusting Sarath, Anil asks for help, only to find herself taken back to Colombo, where she is to give a report in the Armoury Auditorium of the anti-terrorist unit building, the skeleton confiscated as well as her notes. Realizing the danger she is in, Sarath discredits and ridicules her, and suggests putting her to the test on another skeleton. In fact, it is a trick to get her out safe and let her have her notes again so that she will be able to flee the country and take the evidence abroad. The tortured body of Sarath is later identified by his brother, a doctor, during his weekly examination of corpses brought to the hospital, while victims start flowing in after a terrorist attack has killed the President and an unknown number of people on National Heroes Day.

Once again, Ondaatje engages with history, a history that has been materially silenced, and proceeds in its interrogation involving aspects related to geographical discourse and language, with identity as an overarching question, both at local level, as the main cause for conflict, and in its transnational and transgendered dimensions, as embodied by the Sri Lankan-born, Western-educated woman who rejected her name and bought Anil, her brother's unused second name for "one hundred saved rupees, a pen set [...] a tin of fifty Gold Leaf cigarettes [...] and a sexual favour he had demanded in the last hours of the impasse" (*AG*, 68).

The effects of the undeclared war are visible everywhere, with bodies washed ashore, floating in rivers, spiked along roads, emerging in paddy fields, flooding hospital emergency wards, in a geography of violence that seems equally distributed between rural and urban areas, north and south. Apparently the conflict is looked at from a Sinhalese perspective, and one of the main characters, Gamini, captured by Tamil guerrillas in Trincomalee and forced to operate on badly wounded young boys, is even reported thinking:

> Who sent a thirteen-year-old to fight, and for what furious cause? For an old leader? For some pale flag? He had to keep reminding himself who these people were. Bombs on crowded streets, in bus stations, paddy fields. [...] Hundreds of victims had died under Gamini's care [...] Still. He was a doctor. (220)

This partial perspective is however counterbalanced by reports of the bloodshed inflicted on the northern province, where Gamini worked for some years, by comments like "No one from the Ministry of Health had ever come to the border villages"[37] (245), but above all by the sense of threat radiating from Colombo, the centre of power. Of the capital city, "dark with curfew" (75), only institutional facets are seen – the airport, the Archaeological Department, the anti-terrorist unit building, Galle Face Green during the parade on National Heroes Day, Kinsey Road Hospital – places where, in different ways, the war is planned or carried out, where "nothing is anonymous" (72) except political victims. And fear, "a national disease" according to Sarath (53), creeps among people, passing from him, who makes sure Anil's tape recorder is off before answering her question about the President,

---

[37] The internal border, or Forward Defence Line, stretched from Mannar on the west coast, through Vavuniya in the centre, to Batticaloa on the east coast and separated the territory controlled by the government in the south from the LTTE's in the north. For a discussion of the border, see Chapter 2.1.

to Anil herself, who speaks in whispers although she is "six hours away from Colombo" (53).

On the map of violence, the only sanctuaries seem to be the *walawwa*, the house in the hills where Anil, Sarath and Ananda retreat to carry out their identification work, and the forest monasteries scattered all over the country. Despite the non-aggressive connotation of the *walawwa*, given by its being built following criteria that subvert the attitude typical of Western exploration and geographical writing, so that "the careful use of distance [...] – the lack of great views of another person's land – make[s] you turn inward rather than dominate the world around you" (201), peace does not dwell there, as the region has become "rife with disappearances" (164), and the interior strangely displays the words "MAKAMKRUKA" and "MADANARAGA" in huge script on a wall, meaning respectively "a churner, and agitator [...] a devil almost" and "with the speed of love" (165), terms that, however difficult to contextualize, certainly do not evoke peaceful feelings, as Ananda's attempt to stab himself to death will prove.

The forest monasteries raise more complex problems: a retreat for scarred people – like Palipana, whose brother was murdered, and his niece who saw her parents being killed –, they are immersed in a timeless peace which is perceived also by the rational-minded Anil. However, as Tariq Jazeel's essay (2005) suggests, forest monasteries can be read as bearing a much deeper significance within a poetics of landscape that reveals their ideological exploitation in the framework of a racialized cultural politics of identity. Focussing on the character of Palipana, who "was for a number of years at the centre of a nationalistic group that eventually wrestled archaeological authority in Sri Lanka away from the Europeans" (*AG,* 79), Jazeel identifies his real-life model in the government archaeologist Senerat Parnavitarna, who in the 1920s strongly contributed to the inscription of Ceylon's geographical space as a cradle of Sinhala-Buddhist culture. Applying the metaphor of landscape as the inscape of a nation, Parnavitarna helped the Ceylon Archaeological Department to promote racially territorialized identities strictly connected with the way in which the landscape was posited and experienced. In an example of what Homi Bhabha defines "the power of the eye to naturalize the rhetoric of national affiliation and its forms of collective expression" (1994, 143), great effort was devoted to proving the truth of the foundational Sinhala chronicle, the *Mahāvamsa*, by finding in rural landscapes sites that showed remnants of history as portrayed in it, so that a Sinhala heroic past could pre-date the arrival of the Tamils. Parnavitarna's anti-colonial activity also included the translation of Pāli inscriptions through which various kings bequeathed caves to Buddhist monks, thus disowning the right of the British Crown over land which had conveniently been termed *terra nullius*, and preventing at the same time claims by the other ethnic groups of the island.

Similarly, Ondaatje's Palipana, "the main force of a pragmatic Sinhala movement" (*AG,* 79), was engaged in bringing to light a sacred past that also constituted a rhetorical strategy aiming at the definition of the "true" Sri Lankan people, but abandoned the profession following a scandal around some allegedly forged translations and went to live in the Grove of Ascetics, the stone and wood remains of a forest monastery not far from the ancient capital Anuradhapura. The location, the silence, the young girl attending the old and almost blind scholar evoke a sacredness that, enhanced through Palipana's story about the grove being the place where, according to the *Cūlavamsa*, king Udaya killed some fugitive monks, is perceived even by Anil, who bathes at the well with long slow gestures repeated in a kind of mantra. The fact that such sacredness is steeped in nature constitutes "but a short pre-reflective step for these embodied experiences to be objectified as expressions of reality located in the very soil of the land" (Jazeel 2005, 12), which by disrupting the dualism nature/culture would project any built structure as a natural formation and further legitimize the exclusivity of a Sinhala-Buddhist heritage. In this sense, *Anil's Ghost* is also an investigation of those discourse strategies analyzed in Chapter Two that contribute to the creation of history and to its nationalistic turn, deployed in this case in a field where history and geography overlap.

The other prominent geographical element is the self-contained one and a half pages describing the National Atlas of Sri Lanka:

> The National Atlas of Sri Lanka has seventy-three versions of the island – each template revealing only one aspect, one obsession: rainfall, winds, surface water of lakes, rarer bodies of water locked deep within the earth.
>
> The old portraits show the produce and former kingdoms of the country; contemporary portraits show levels of wealth, poverty and literacy.
>
> The geological map reveals peat in the Muthurajawela swamp south of Negombo, coral along the coast from Ambalangoda to Dondra Head, pearl banks offshore in the Gulf of Mannar...
>
> There are no city names. [...] There are no river names. No depiction of human life. (*AG*, 39-40)

Thus sectioned, the country becomes a repertoire of facts that completely obliterate human presence. This pageant of Western taxonomies, which also exemplifies Mary Louise Pratt's contention (1992) that Linné's classification boosted the interest in new lands by marking on maps the raw materials available, is read by Jazeel as Ondaatje fictionally replicating the real-life National Atlas of Sri Lanka, whose section on "Ancient Cities and Settlements" states that "although the presence of humankind in Sri Lanka probably dates from around 75,000 years ago, Sri Lanka's 'Historical Epoch' begins only from 250 years BCE" (Jazeel 2005, 15). As the time period indicated here corresponds to King Devanampiya Tissa's conversion to Buddhism, the union of what can be termed "history" and today's state religion creates a strong entity that sweeps aside thousands of years by making them pre-historical, hence delegitimizing any group except the Sinhala-Buddhist at a very crucial time, since the Atlas was authorized by the state in 1988, still in the wake of the civil war of 1983.

While this provides illuminating insights into the socio-historical context, I would also point out how, on a textual level, this section is immediately followed by a list of people reported as missing, drawn, as Ondaatje states in his acknowledgements, from Amnesty International reports. The last line in the Atlas section, stressing the absence of human life, is doubly linked to the apparently detached next page: if on the one hand the void left on maps is filled by naming – and hence calling into existence – people, on the other hand their absence is bitterly ascertained through precisely the same means: human life is written but still absent, actually absent *because* written, which creates a potential, paradoxical connection between Amnesty International's reports and the "list of government undesirables" (*AG*, 269).

As, however, it is mainly by hinting at the responsibilities of historical and political discourse that *Anil's Ghost* engages with the tragic consequences of a civil war caused by identity and territory claims, the mutually supportive actions of language (with translation as one of its dimensions) and history need to be looked into from exactly the same perspective, that is, by considering how the two are set to work in the text.

In a country where "everyone was vaguely related and had Sinhalese, Tamil, Dutch, British and Burgher blood" (*RF*, 41), language becomes the most evident ethnic marker, the one that no longer identifies Anil Tissera, as from the very start she announces she only speaks "a little" Sinhala (*AG*, 9). The elusive nature of Anil's identity emerges through her rejection of both her previous self, the one she was known by in Sri Lanka – a swimmer who gained a headline in *The Observer* having won the yearly two-mile competition by the Mount Lavinia Hotel – and the reference to it implied in the phrase "the return of the prodigal" (10). The woman identified by a British passport "with the light-blue UN bar" (9) had progressively severed her connections to the island in the years before: the distance created when she started studying in England increased with her parents' death in a car accident, with the divorce from a Sri Lankan husband met in London, and with her move to America, following a personal evolution that led her to embrace more and more the West, its anonymity, its scientific approach to research, its language. The return to Sri Lanka, following an application halfheartedly sent to the Centre for Human Rights in Geneva, is accompanied by a detached attitude acquired in the years abroad, when she learnt "to interpret Sri Lanka with a long-distance gaze" (11), but at the same time by the awareness that "suddenly [...] the buried senses from childhood [were] alive in her" (15), a gut feeling that materializes in her first requests – toddy, curd and jaggery.

The persona entering Sri Lanka is the result of a process of estrangement whereby the young girl "confused by the geography around her" (141) during her first month in London, desperately missing her native language and food, emerged from the ruins of a marriage dictated by homesickness and by the need to intimately share a familiar past. For all his reassuring familiarity, the husband, who metonymically stood for her native country, soon began interfering with her choices, so that Anil – who, we are told, likes privacy and doing things on her own terms – had to terminate the relationship and simultaneously cut all links with her previous life. Thus, after speaking Sinhala for the last time during "the distressed chat she'd had with Lalitha that ended with her crying about missing egg *rulang* and curd with jaggery" (145), she never pronounced her husband's name, nor spoke Sinhala to anyone. The passage from the language of emotions to the language of reason was fully accomplished by diving into study, "practically memorizing Spitz and Fisher" till she "was [...] alongside the language of science" (*ibid.*), examples of which appear in her next relationship, when she boasts "I know the names of several bones in Spanish" (34). Language, then, becomes a means to recreate oneself, an auto-translation corresponding to phases of life and the selves one impersonates: Sinhala for the young swimmer fond of jaggery, English for the transnational woman used to dissecting corpses.

English, however, makes Anil a foreigner in Sri Lanka, a "woman from Geneva", as entomologist Chitra Abeysekera greets her, who has hardly any ability to truly communicate with locals. Visiting her old *ayah* Lalitha, Anil feels that "there was a lost language between them" (22), a language temporarily replaced by touch and weeping, but not opening the doors of belonging for Anil, further closed off by Lalitha's granddaughter speaking Tamil to the old woman and not offering to translate into or from English. After courting foreignness in the West, Anil feels that she is "moving with only one arm of language among uncertain laws and a fear that was everywhere" (54). This first realization of the difficulty of applying the "clearly marked roads to the source of most mysteries" (*ibid.*) learnt in the course of her Western education is a meditation on the weight and dangerousness of the spoken word, able to citizen or to isolate her, and on her need to rely on Sarath to make up for her maimed ability. Thus, it is Sarath who explains to the man found crucified on the road that she is a doctor, just as it is him again Anil asks for help when, struck by the realization that she has forgotten "the subtleties of the language they once shared" (170), she needs to communicate with the artist Ananda. While touch mediates for Anil's muted tongue – kissing Lalitha, holding Gunesena's wounded hands while squeezing salty water on them, touching Ananda's forearm in agreement – and, in Palipana's case, for his blind eyes, it also represents a movement toward tuning in to local conventions, regaining confidence with the indefiniteness of the recurring Asian nod, "which included in its almost circular movement the possibility of a no" (16-17). As Sandeep Sanghera points out, "nothing is said directly and that is the Sri

Lankan language of subtleties" (2004, 3), a code Anil has to translate herself into, and convert her obsession for straight-line truth into an oblique, circular, approach – the same kind of approach that Sarath, resorting to artistic reconstruction, adopts as a complement to her scientific tests to identify the skeleton. For Anil, this means letting go of her belief that "meaning allowed a person a door to escape grief and fear" and realizing that "those who were slammed and stained by violence lost the power of language and logic" (*AG*, 55), which is what helps her to accept the nonverbal quality of Sarath, Gamini, Gunesena, and especially Ananda, all touched by violence albeit in different ways. To them, steeped in the country's dramatic events, Anil's search for truth sounds impossible in a Western perspective and obscenely connoted in contemporary Sri Lankan terms because of the torture and massacre deployed to pursue it. As J. U. Jacobs observed during a seminar at Turin University in January 2003, in terror regimes truth is a pre-existing idea in the mind of the interrogator for which he seeks verification, and he does so by applying the assumption that pain is truth. If physical pain shatters the language by reverting it to inarticulate sounds, it can be assumed that emotional pain, or grief for a missing family member, affects it too. Writing on the discovery of mass graves and unidentified skeletal remains in the south of Sri Lanka, sociologist Sasanka Perera argues:

> experiences of unnatural and violent death (particularly those involving the absence of a body) and the narratives of such experiences have to be understood in the context of a language of incompleteness, suddenness, darkness, and endless unfulfilled continuity. (1999, 4)

Although charged with different meaning – a key to access truth for Anil, a more emotional response for those who have been to some degree involved in the politics of terror – Ananda's reconstruction of the skeleton's face marks a turning point that shifts balances. The face is infused with the peace that Ananda wishes for his wife, who disappeared in the wake of group killings of students; finally having a fetish of her corpse, he can let the long-repressed grief flood him, but the depth of it induces him to attempt suicide. Moved by the revelations about Ananda's wife, Anil adopts a more compassionate attitude in her search, even asking Sarath not to show the head in the villages around to spare the inhabitants a re-lived trauma. But it is Ananda stabbing himself (significantly in the throat, as if to eliminate the possibility of speaking) that completes Anil's re-rooting in her country, for, after medicating him provisionally, she feels "she could speak in any language, he would understand the purpose of any gesture" (*AG,* 197), and when he is driven to hospital by Sarath, Anil, alone in the *walawwa,* is finally able to rest:

> She was with Sarath and Ananda, citizened by their friendship – the two of them in the car, the two of them in the hospital while a stranger attempted to save Ananda. (200)

The newly acquired language of citizenship is what Sarath hears during her report before government officials:

> It was a lawyer's argument and, more important, a citizen's evidence; she was no longer a foreign authority. Then he heard her say, "I think you murdered hundreds of us." *Hundreds of us.* Sarath thought to himself. Fifteen years away and she is finally *us.* (271-72)

Ironically, it is the move back into citizenship that forces her out of the country to find shelter after the dangerous revelations, but above all to become a spokesperson for those fellow citizens who have been silenced, thus giving substance to her claim that "one victim can speak for many victims" (176).

***

As in his earlier books, Ondaatje relies on fragments to be reconstructed, more than ever replicating in the form the pattern of research that is the core of the novel, and frequently deploying those ruptures in time typical of postmodernist writing[38] that reject the unifying flow of the individual mind and reproduce instead the suspensions and abrupt shifts induced by dramatic conditions or, as Margaret Scanlan contends, "create a sense of time experienced through terror, by people living in fear that they can be blown away in an instant, to whom historical perspective is a luxury" (2004, 303).

While pointing out that he does not want the novel to be "taken as representative"[39] nor to give the ultimate version of the story, Ondaatje is careful not to transform it into an aestheticized parable of terror by providing contextualizing information in his Author's Note:

> From the mid-1980s to the early 1990s, Sri Lanka was in a crisis that involved three essential groups: the government, the antigovernment insurgents in the south and the separatist guerrillas in the north. [...] legal and illegal government squads were known to have been sent out to hunt down the separatists and the insurgents.
>
> *Anil's Ghost* is a fictional work set during this political time and historical moment.

History is explicitly thematized and explores a tragic situation still deeply ingrained in Sri Lanka. The desire to refrain from "the usual journalistic contemporary situation, where you read in the paper that three bombs have gone off, and people forget about it ten minutes later",[40] is mirrored in a narration that, without advancing any political theory or indulging in the sensationalism of gruesome violence,

---

[38] "Chronoschisms" in Ursula Heise's terms (quoted in Margaret Scanlan 2004, 303).

[39] Interview, "M. Ondaatje in Conversation with M. Jaggi", *Wasafiri* 32 (Autumn 2000): 5-11.

[40] Ondaatje's words as reported in Peter Coughlan's "Meander, If You Want to Get to Town", a conversation with the author after being awarded the Kiriyama Book Prize 2000, available at www.kiriyamaprize.org.

succeeds in honouring the victims and indicting the establishment through the commitment of the main characters.

Since the particular circumstances of Sri Lankan politics in those years seem, as Scanlan contends,

> to reflect back postmodern notions of the collapse of grand narratives, the fragility and impermanence of identity, the failure of history to provide us with a coherent account of our origins, and the moral ambiguities of action and character in a world where cause and effect are endlessly complex (2004, 303-4),

Ondaatje keeps the novel grounded by using facts as his subtext: by referring to mass graves and killings that, as Amnesty International among others reported, were part of Sri Lankan life in the late 80s and early 90s, by including actual archaeological sites, by having the fictional president killed in circumstances that echo the death of president Ranasinghe Premedasa in 1993 and by providing plenty of culture-specific information often left untranslated.

If, as Foucault contends, "history is one way in which a society recognizes and develops a mass of documentation with which it is inextricably linked" (2004, 7), the problem *Anil's Ghost* raises is that of a fracture between the way history is presented and what Sri Lankan society is ready to recognize. The fracture acquires further ramifications depending on epoch, for while ancient history is construed so as to fulfil a nationalistic purpose and is absorbed unquestioningly by large sections of the population thanks to its recourse to aesthetics and art, contemporary history – largely a result of nationalist rhetoric – meets society's disbelief as the countless corpses found all over the country expose contradicting versions resulting from the connection between the sources of history and power. History is then posited as a convenient reordering of chaos, if not a lie. Ondaatje, however, questions history and its methods of interrogation, but does not subscribe to one particular approach nor to its spokesperson. So, while suggesting that an interrogative relationship to the earth – in the sense of both the landscape and the sedimentation of traces in the layers of soil – might hold a key to retrieve pre-existing realities, the novel proceeds to show basically two investigative ways: Anil's positivistic approach, trusting that through science "truth comes finally into the light" because "it's in the bones and sediment" (*AG*, 259), and Sarath's slower pace in search of narratives: "Someone nudges a stone away and there's a story" (*ibid.*). This oversimplification, however, is nuanced by Anil's realization that in Sri Lanka "truth bounced between gossip and vengeance" (54) and by the slippery contours of Sarath and especially of Palipana, highly committed to historical and archaeological research, as well as embodying "authentic" post-colonial points of view. Besides being based on his exhaustive research and deep knowledge, Palipana's former reputation was supported by his efforts to – as Dipesh Chakrabarty (1995) would say – "provincialize Europe":

> While the West saw Asian history as a faint horizon where Europe joined the East, Palipana saw his country in fathoms and colour, and Europe simply as a landmass on the end of the peninsula of Asia. (*AG*, 79)

Palipana's scepticism allows Ondaatje to be ironical about supposed universal truths dating back to social Darwinism and Orientalism:

> Academics flew into Delhi, Colombo and Hong Kong for six days, told their best anecdotes, took the pulse of the ex-colony, and returned to London and Boston. It was finally realized that while European culture was old, Asian culture was older. (*ibid.*)

The passage also echoes Yasmine Gooneratne's reflections (1980) on the link between the label "Third World" and the impossibility for

Asian cultures to explicitly state their ancient roots as the term "Old World" was appropriated by Europe after Columbus' journey to America, which by contrast became the New World.

Palipana, the blind scholar, reads history as it is narrated by stone and memory. Contrary to the Western tradition, the most authoritative figure to guide historical research is not endowed with the dominant power of the eye: although he says that "without the eyes there is not just blindness, there is nothing. There is no existence" (*AG*, 99), his own response to losing the power of vision is a greater freedom from the fixed boundaries of the visible, which allows him to link past, present, art, life, history and myth and create a mode of perceiving the world which is juxtaposed to the compartmentalized maps in the Archaeological Office. This eager scholar, a model for his students, was apparently endowed with the perfect blend of knowledge and passion, for "he knew the languages and the techniques of research better than those above him" (80), and at the same time "he approached runes not with a historical text but with the pragmatic awareness of locally inherited skills" (82), setting moreover great value on memory, aware as he was that "history faded too, as much as battles did, and [...] could exist only with remembrance" (104). Palipana is shown as a potentially ideal spokesperson for the postmodern and post-colonial questioning of historical discourse: as "in the last few years he had found the hidden histories, intentionally lost, that altered the perspective and knowledge of earlier times" (105), he is aware of its narrative dimension, but the initial alarming hint at his nationalistic fervour is compounded by his falling in disgrace following accusations of forgery. "He had discovered and translated a linguistic subtext that explained the political tides and royal eddies of the island in the sixth century" (81), but no evidence of the source was ever found. In a significant mesh of history and translation, the underlying aim is once again to focus on the production of historical knowledge; thus, while Palipana's work was acclaimed, the absence of the texts he was supposed to have translated led to the acknowledgement that "they were a fiction" (81). To further disrupt clear-cut judgements, such a strong statement is then mitigated by an exploration of the possible reasons behind his act: as Palipana was known as "the strictest of historians" (*ibid.*), the hypothesis is advanced that "for him it was not a false step but the step to another reality, the last stage of a long, truthful dance" (*ibid.*), and "he began to see as truth things that could only be guessed at" (83). What emerges from this problematization of history is not an indication of the path to follow, but rather a warning about the scientific exploration that finds its expressions in both Anil's studying dead tissue and in the "Very Large Array of Telescopes, which minute by minute drew information out of the skies. Information about the state of things ten billion years ago, and as many miles out" (255), as well as caution about an approach that in its attempt to overthrow dominant modes (here Western taxonomies and colonial constructs) rejects them and in so doing ends up with other constructs, different only in that they endorse a particularistic discourse, that is, nationalism and the internal colonialism it promotes toward minorities. Both methods present dangers, both reduce human presence to inert material, to "a detail from the subplot" (256), both erase memory, as the Alzheimer's affecting Anil's American friend Leaf and the nameless, forgotten victims in Sri Lanka hint at.

While the scanty reference to colonialism or to the West carries some criticism, there is no concession to nativistic idealization: thus, the removal of the Bodhisattvas by Japanese archaeologists and the following purchase by museums in the West finds its counterpart in three locals destroying the stone Buddha, while Palipana's fascinating suggestion to have the face of the skeleton reconstructed by the artificer Ananda does not work in itself, but will – almost esoterically – lead to the identification of Ruwan Kumara through Anil's recognition of the same occupation markers in both.

The nuancing of opposites and the very fields touched upon in *Anil's Ghost* remind of Foucault's statement:

> There was a time when archaeology [...] aspired to the condition of history, and attained meaning only through the restitution of a historical discourse; [...] in our time history aspires to the condition of archaeology, to the intrinsic description of the monument. (2004, 8)

A symbolical instance of Foucault's suggestion that history today transforms documents into monuments might be seen in the passage from human rights reports to the monument to human life that is the unknown skeleton and the countless anonymous victims with him, but the link between the two fields of knowledge is made more explicit by emphasizing in-depth investigations, fathoming and digging as a *leitmotiv* introduced from the very start with the miner's folk song and the excavations in Guatemala that prelude Anil's arrival in Sri Lanka, indicating that that is the way to follow in order to – layer after layer – get closer to truth.

A two-level movement occurs as the investigations conducted to identify the skeleton also allow excursions into the island's complex past and draw attention to the problem of representation as well as the importance of the point of view. This is why Sarath requires Anil to "understand the archaeological surround of a fact" (*AG*, 44) and overcome the detached attitude she has acquired in the West, which risks to make her see things as "those journalists who file reports about flies and scabs while staying at the Galle Face Hotel. That false empathy and blame" (*ibid.*). The preoccupation with representation is reiterated in the thoughts and words of both brothers:

> Sarath had seen truth broken into suitable pieces and used by the foreign press alongside irrelevant photographs. A flippant gesture towards Asia that might lead, as a result of this information, to new vengeance and slaughter. (156-57)

'American movies, English books – remember how they all end?' Gamini asked that night. 'the American or the

Englishman gets on a plane and leaves. That's it. The camera leaves with him. [. . .] He's going home. So the war, to all purposes, is over. That's enough reality for the West.' (285-86).

While in response to Sarath's concern with truth the novel abounds with references to how provisional, dangerous and one-sided truth can be, Gamini's summary of Anglo-American cultural portraits seems to be confirmed at first, with the information that Anil *will* actually get on a plane and leave, but it is then subverted twice – for this is not, or no longer, a Western narrative – through a gaze that does not follow the departure of the hero(ine), but stays on to reveal the tragic consequences of Sarath's pursuit of truth, and then moves out to show a collective effort to recompose a Buddha which had been blown up, not out of the iconoclastic fury that scarred Afghanistan, but by three thieves who hoped to find a treasure inside. The image of the restoration of the Buddha evokes the salvific power of art – literally, since Ananda resorts to recruiting villagers to save them from being pulled into the army or rounded up as suspects – through community work in a newly found religious, historical and generational continuity.

The structure of the novel replicates its internal turning points: as Anil has to re-find her language of belonging before she can dig into Sri Lankan history, so Ondaatje had to immerse himself in the past of his country to revive the link of citizenship, which is what has allowed him, although writing from without, to adopt a sympathetic perspective and provide a transnational narrative that goes beyond established patterns.

4.2 Carl Muller: Within and About Sri Lanka

Born and living in Sri Lanka, Carl Muller is a prolific writer and a journalist well-known in his native country, in India and Australia for the saga of the Von Bloss family – *The Jam Fruit Tree* (1993), *Yakada*

Yakā (1994) and *Once Upon a Tender Time* (1995)[41] – and for his satire and extreme outspokenness. Muller too belongs to the minority known as Burghers, but because he has remained in Sri Lanka, the ethnic label has a much stronger impact than for Ondaatje. Somewhat displaced even in their native country, the Burghers have been "positioned as the 'degenerate outsider' in pre-independence nationalist discourses and, in the post-independence landscape, as a continuing reminder of colonialism" (Silva 2004a, 104). Thus, Muller occupies a peculiar position on the Sri Lankan literary scene: white, with English as his mother tongue, in the Author's Note to *Colombo* he writes "I am a Sri Lankan and this land of my birth is very dear to me" (ix), yet he experiences daily the relevance of ethnicity in his country: "If I go to the hospital for a blood test, I'm given a form to fill in, and on the line 'nationality' I can't write 'Sri Lankan', I have to write 'Burgher', otherwise I won't be accepted".[42] Even in critical appraisal of his works there seems to be a need to point out "Burgherness": as Dushyanthi Mendis argues, Muller is both a post-independence and a post-colonial writer since he "writes about the Burghers [...] whose origins coincide with and are inextricably linked to the years of Portuguese and Dutch colonies in the country" (1998, 64). Similarly, having English as his mother tongue – after the privilege it conferred under the British and the stigma it raised immediately after independence – is today recognized as a valuable tool that however needs to be constantly bridged through translation. Language, then, is one of the aspects Muller works on in his writing, not by reflecting on its processes, but by using it in ways that on the

---

[41] A fourth book, *Spit and Polish* (1998), traces the adventures of Carloboy von Bloss, but because the family is eclipsed and the text alternates narrative chapters focused on Carloboy's experience in the Navy with chapters devoted to the Second World War in the Pacific area, it is usually considered separately, whereas the three preceding novels are referred to as "the Burgher trilogy" (Walker 1998; Sarvan 1997). In parenthetical reference hereafter they will appear as *JFT*, *YY* and *OUTT*.

[42] Personal conversation with the author (Kandy, April 1, 2005).

one hand show a departure from Standard English and on the other mock its usage by the various communities.

The other two dimensions, geography and history, are strictly intertwined and often referred to in relation to European presence on the island; but it is especially history that frequently appears in the narrative, either as an explicit meditation on the past or as implied reference in dialogues. While, coherently with the overall tone, geography and history are dealt with ironically in the Burgher trilogy, in *Colombo: A Novel* (1995) sarcasm and bitterness characterize the city-text.

4.2.1 *The Jam Fruit Tree, Yakada Yakā, Once Upon a Tender Time*: Bittersweet Scenes of a "madcap, merry lifestyle."

Muller's trilogy looks back into the vanished subculture of the Burghers by tracing the lives of three generations of a lower middle class family in the twentieth century through a semi-autobiographical narration where "the backdrop is fact, the centre stage fiction, sometimes exchanged, transposed" (*OUTT*, xiii). Although they can be read as self-contained texts, the books form a sequel: thus, *The Jam Fruit Tree* follows the ups and downs of Cecilprins von Bloss' large family through the marriages, fights and careers of the eight children; *Yakada Yakā* focuses on Sonnaboy von Bloss, the youngest son, and his adventures as an engine driver in the Ceylon Railway, while *Once Upon a Tender Time* narrates the childhood and youth of his son Carloboy. It is especially the last two books which draw more heavily on autobiographical experience and constitute, as Muller – somewhat echoing Nietzsche – states, "work[s] of faction [...] more fact than fiction, if you please, but that will always remain, I suppose, a matter of personal interpretation" (*YY*, 2).

In spite of the continuity provided by the main characters, the texts read more like a series of sketches, with sequences that portray the countless episodes and meetings of everyday life and celebrate the alcoholic and sexual excesses of the vigorous Burgher culture of old

Sri Lanka. The comedic tone fits Yasmine Gooneratne's identification of wry humour as characteristic of storytelling in Southeast Asia (1979) and creates a very distinctive, at times extravagant, narrative voice that plays on words and often depicts grotesque images. Despite the entertainment the books provide, Muller's primary aim seems to be that of establishing a distinctive identity for the Burghers, thus confirming to a certain degree the weight of those political and social developments that Nagesh Rao defines "the inexorable processes of ethnicisation in post-independence Sri Lanka" (quoted in Perera 2000, 14).

Keenly aware of the debate around history and fiction, in "Historical fiction: The Historical Sensibility of the Story-Teller" (*The Island*) Muller claims that "if fiction can spring from history, then this fiction can also reshape popular conceptions of the past", which is a way of looking at the trilogy in its attempt to redefine the Burghers, their presence on the island and their disintegration as a result of increasingly nationalistic post-independence policies. In spite of the differences, the picture that emerges reminds of *Running in the Family*, a similarity Muller himself acknowledges:

> Michael Ondaatje dipped into his family's past in *Running in the Family*. I tried that too, and have been run out of the family – and again, so what? What we must own is the writer's power to reconstruct and inhabit a space in time past. (*ibid.*)

The overabundant definitions of Burgherness are produced either through explicit interventions by the chronicler, who every now and then refers to their origins, their attitude to life, their relation to Sri Lanka and to the other communities of the island, or through dialogues where history and language mix and are acted out as the stories unfold. Thus, the Von Blosses are described as "all in all a robust, brawny, bawdy family, praising the Lord, church-going, singing their Aves with the same gusto as they would eat, drink and fornicate" (*JFT*, 7), and the Burghers in general "took life easy and never troubled themselves with high intent or purpose", showing an attitude of "eat, drink and be merry and to Hades with tomorrow!" (*YY*, 114-15). At the same time, as the narrator says, "they were adaptable and as hardy as the cockroach [...] and they believed in living life to the full" (*JFT*, 28), which as Vasuki Walker points out, is an example of appropriating a derogatory term used in reference to the Burghers by the other communities and subverting it for positive effect (1998, 92).

The boundaries of this ethnic group vary according to the point of view: indeed, there is a certain vagueness in concept, whereby strictly speaking the Burghers are "the descendants of male European settlers under the Dutch East India company" (Mendis 1998, 64), but in the twentieth century the label was applied to people of both Dutch and Portuguese origins, and in its broadest sense it has come to include all those of sundry European and local ancestry. There is, however, a double perception within the group itself which, acknowledging a certain closeness to European culture, tends to stick to its own kind and at the same time feels ostracized by the other communities; conversely, the rest of Sri Lankan society has mixed feelings toward the Burghers, ranging from mild statements of otherness to aggressive delegitimization. Thus, borrowing Said's notion of repetition, Charles Sarvan claims that "what [...] finally made the Burghers a community was [...] their consciousness of forming a distinct group, [...] and they perpetuated this identity by contracting marriages within the group" (2001, 527), while Neluka Silva reports the spiteful attitude of early nationalists:

> In 1982, Anagrika Dharmapala identified the Burghers as the "hybrids and bastards of Sinhalese who have become traitors to the country, honoured with Christian names, given ranks and made leaders of society." (2004a, 104)

The charge of immorality is raised especially against women, who, in contradiction to Sarvan's statement, are believed to be promiscuous, ready to resort to sex to improve their position in society and eagerly trying to marry into other groups so as to erase their allegedly shameful origins (Silva 2004a).

Given such controversial attitudes, it is easier to understand Muller's need to substantiate identity claims. From the very start of the trilogy, the Burghers are set apart from the native Sinhalese, who "were a pretty insular lot" (*JFT*, 26) and included in a loosely defined mix deriving from the Portuguese and the Dutch, who "found Sinhalese and Tamil girls to their liking", and from the British, who "went in among the natives too", thus creating a "hotch-potch [...] further spiced by other foreign types who drifted in and out [...] French, Germans, Persians, Indians, Afghans [...] and Scandinavians" (*JFT*, 27). After such "merry-go-round" beginnings, the Burghers are portrayed as entitled to their place in the country, "as native as the most strident Sinhala native" (*JFT*, 137):

> They knew how to fit in, to belong. They accepted, centuries ago, that Sri Lanka was their land. There was never any thought that they could, if things got bad, pack and hie back to Holland or to wherever they could trace back to. They were at home, and where else could they "put a party" and enjoy life as much as at home? (*ibid.*)

The sense of belonging to the place is undermined, however, by a degree of uncertainty that in other points of the novels posits the Sinhalese as the "authentic" people of Sri Lanka, a view that contradicts the confidence shown above. This mainly happens on occasions when, either directly or through the unfolding of events, reference is made to the privilege the Burghers enjoyed in colonial times, almost an acknowledgement of their indirect participation in the inequality of the system prompted by what may be considered a sense of guilt: tracing their origins back to the sixteenth and seventeenth centuries does not seem to be enough to erase their sense of being a temporary presence on the island and, what is more, a not too justifiable one:

> The Burghers found immense favour with the British [...] they were regarded as those of "European descent", posed no communication problem and were a far cry over the Sinhalese who were of ill-disposition, morose, apt to fawn and bootlick and then do a Brutus. So it was that while the true people of Ceylon, the Sinhalese, were the subject race, the hewers of wood and drawers of water, the vast contingent of Burghers, all nondescript, no-roots, fair-skinned hybrids, became the white-collar workers, the police inspectors, the fire chiefs, foremen, storekeepers, managers [...] and formed an upper stratum in the social hierarchy. (*JFT,* 28)

> Civil servants from Madras, well schooled in their work, were shipped in . . . and this caused more problems. [...] The Burghers continued to be "looked after". The Sinhalese, tragically, were left out in the cold . . . and this, tragically too, was their land. (*OUTT,* 14)

These are expressions of the uneasiness deriving from occupying the margin between British power and wealth and Sinhalese disenfranchisement, from being neither the fully empowered conqueror nor the rooted native, a kind of middle level between the ruler and the ruled, the foreigner and the native. The intermittent claim to Sri Lankan citizenship might also be due to the lack of a consolidated cultural heritage to be proud of or to identify with, as – differently from both the Sinhalese and the Tamils – the Burghers have no ancient ruins or landscape to mythologize, but only structures that inevitably recall colonialism and therefore represent in collective memory emotionally charged sites. As a matter of fact, the Burghers in the trilogy hardly appear to have any link with nature and the landscape: usually moving in urban areas, they face life's vicissitudes within domestic spaces, on the workplace, between the workplace and home. Only in *Yakada Yakā*, which as the title promises[43] deals with Burgher railwaymen, does Sonnaboy von Bloss travel around the country, sometimes to rather isolated settlements, where however the Burghers always manage to find a place for drinking and partying. The transfer to Anuradhapura, for example, opens with a short neutral introduction to the sacred city that "holds the ruins of an ancient Buddhist civilization" (129), but its status is immediately downsized: "It was the first capital of Sri Lanka with kings who had a high old time until the Buddha sent an emissary from India to show them the error of their ways" (*ibid.*). Alternating temples and dynasties to malaria and invaders, and finally panning in on a locomotive yard, the narrator (rather simplistically) deconstructs the grandeur and the reasons for pride of the ruined city:

> In Sri Lanka today, people still hark back to the glories of the past and the wonders wrought by the kings of old. They forget to mention that they allowed it all to go to pot because they don't like to admit that they have always needed someone to rub their noses to the grindstone. [...] The Portuguese cashed in on this indolence to wield sword and bible. The Dutch sought to put the house in order with ledger and lawbook, while the British decided that if they were to continue to be shopkeepers (they always are), they needed the commercial infrastructure: roads, railways and the grabbing of every bit of land for the planting of coffee and tea and rubber. (*YY*, 129-30)

The lightness of the tone in reviewing such important events and the evident rejection of politically correct discourse do not dispel,

---

[43] "When the conquering British rolled out the first railway steam-driven locomotive on iron rails in Sri Lanka, it caused quite a stir. [...] This Thing, the villagers declared, was an Iron Demon – a *yakada yakā*" (*YY*, i).

however, the impression that the narrator misses a glorious past to root himself; on the other hand, while his criticism of the Sinhalese almost sounds like an apology for colonialism, the summary of European methods and aims may also reveal an acknowledgement of their power, but it certainly signals a scornful separation from them too.

The controversial, yet wished for, link to the physicality of the island is perhaps best symbolized by two maps. The railway map beside the frontispiece of *Yakada Yakā*, which only shows Sri Lanka's railway lines and stations echoes Ondaatje's seventy-three templates "revealing only one aspect, one obsession" (*AG*, 39), is tellingly placed at the beginning of the novel Muller dedicates "to the memory of [his] father, Vernon Muller, who, for forty years, drove the Iron Demons in Sri Lanka". In *Once Upon a Tender Time*, instead, the island is transfigured by young Carloboy (Muller's fictional self), who during a geography lesson draws a map of Ceylon standing on two legs and slightly more rounded on the right side with the caption "My mummy going to have a baby", an actual sketch inserted in the novel after being retrieved – a footnote explains – "from the home of Mr Baptiss",[44] (*OUTT*, 182). The overlaying of parental figures and Ceylon might then be read as symbolic of the ambiguous relationship to the father(land)/mother(land) that the author experienced in his personal and social life.

Critical of the local writing tradition that dips its bucket in the "village wells",[45] Muller refrains from endowing rural areas with the

---

44 While the episode might well belong to the realm of "facts", its fictional dimension reminds of Rushdie's "human geography" when Saleem's face embodies the map of India in *Midnight Children* (1995, 231-32). Moreover, given Muller's swaying between fact and fiction and his love for wordplay, one might doubt the authenticity of the source of the retrieval, whose name shows a suspicious closeness to the baptism certainly awaiting newborns in Christian families.

45 The phrase was borrowed from Gamini Haththotuwegama, who used it during a lecture at the 1998 Conference of the Sri Lankan Association of Commonwealth Literature and Language Studies, Oct. 10-12, University of Peradeniya.

idyllic or orientalist attractions found in earlier writing and, on the few occasions where the countryside appears, it features as a backward place of toil:

> Village life in Sri Lanka begins when the first dagger is pushed through the toga of the night, giving the sun a glimpse in at a sleeping world. This, one supposes, is the crack of dawn. [...] The crows hail the hour with their raucous cries [...] Boys are up and about too, since village homes tick along on the energy of the youngsters in this first magic hour. There's firewood to gather and cattle sheds to be cleaned, cows and goats to milk and reed grass cut and sheaved for cattle fodder. [...] All so charming and rustic, don't you think? (*YY*, 147)

In this specific instance, moreover, the rural setting is only described to provide a sharp contrast with two Burgher railwaymen who stopped their train along the line at night and, mightily drunk, went for a swim in one of the highly celebrated traditional water tanks of the northern region; then, stark naked, they fell asleep in the woods, only to wake up the following morning surrounded by a crowd:

> When a bevy of village lassies with their pots and pans saw Sonnaboy and Meerwald, gloriously naked and sleeping like the babes in the wood, they wrung their hands, dropped whatever they were carrying and goggled. Men with their cattle joined the throng and gaped. Never such a sight in all the generations past. Meerwald, white-skinned and positively grotesque with a paunch that beggared description, had rolled to the ground and lay like Moby Dick. [...]
>
> The sight was too much for the rustics. [...] One worthy who decided that something had to be done, threw a stone. (*YY*, 148)

While neither party is spared ridicule, it is the presumably dark-skinned crowd (by contrast with Meerwald's whiteness) that is described in a patronizing tone (village lassies, rustics) and connoted as narrow-minded and aggressive, thus providing one of the many instances of the opposition between "us" and "them" in the three texts.

The differences between ethnic communities are in fact repeatedly highlighted through episodes that are meant to reflect the stereotypical image each holds of the other. In Muller's trilogy the Sinhalese and Tamils are hardly characters, but rather caricatures who, in their subordinate positions – servants like Poddi, gullible Tamil stationmasters, hired mourners – are meant to play second fiddle to and allow the protagonists to reveal particular traits. They are generally kept outside the family clan, except for Colontota, Anna's suitor, who is first ridiculed because of his gaudy European clothes and the highly formal letter he writes to Anna's father in order to introduce himself, and then almost rejected by an incredulous Cecilprins:

> "I want to marry her. I am important man in radio station. Good post. Accounts section. Have property. Have another small house in Battaramulla also. You come anytime you feel like it and see my house."
>
> Cecilprins stared. "You are – you are Sinhalese," he croaked.
>
> "But I am like you people. Educated good and Cambridge Senior also. [...]"
>
> "But my daughter cannot marry a Sinhalese. We are Burgher people, no? How to face if I gave our Anna to a Sinhalese? Funny thing, no? Walking in sarong all over house and putting wooden clogs and going to temple . . . my God, going to temple! You are Buddhist, no? (*JFT*, 35-36)

It is interesting to notice how the dialogue displays on the one hand perfect civility and on the other deep-rooted prejudice that, although neither knows how to justify, informs the exchange. The narrator, however, redresses the balance by pointing out that the Burghers are no longer so fussy, and that "the intermixing today has become something quite fierce and a whole generation of Nathanielszes with Aryan eyes and Dravid lips bear witness to the undoubtedly Sri Lankan connection" (*JFT*, 29).

All through the trilogy, the Burghers emerge as rather superficial and disrespectful but basically harmless; the Sinhalese are often referred to as being lazy and exploitative, while the Tamils – maybe closer to the Burghers given their minority status – are also ridiculed, but figure as hardworking, spiteful of the Burghers for their thoughtlessness, and intent on making money:

> The Tamils, who called the north home, made the best of both worlds. They would come among the Sinhalese in the south, live with them, set up in business, milk the south of all they could and maintain their homes in the north as well. (*YY*, 154)

But the most evident strategy used to portray – and make fun of – Sinhalese and Tamils is through language. Thus, a conversation between two Tamil speakers of English unfolds as follows:

> "Not so rich, my younger brother, but his wife has money. I vill rite and ask if vant to give the daughter."
> John was much obliged but asked, "Vy iss she not married yif nineteen ears?"
> "Because she wanted to study. Vary bright girl. Make good vife for you."
> "Ven riting ask to send a picture, ah?", John suggested.
> "You vait. I vill yarrange if I can." (*YY*, 45)

And a solicitous father would thus show his care:

> Papa Vythialingam would tell his son: "Rajah, *eppudi*? Whair you are going? To play with the cricket bat? Good, good. But cum early back, ah? Do leetle more study in the yevening. Only batanball vand do. See that Burgher pallow nex' door. Hole time on bicycle and going here an' there. Not doing yeny study. And see his father. Just becoze Burgher have job in the Yexcise. But vat for? Nothing to show. Yeverytime saying no money no money. Vee are thinking about future."
> (*YY*, 155)

Tamil speakers of English are mainly identified in the novels through phonetic deviation: hence the problematic pronunciation of the phoneme [w], which is either elided ("rite" instead of "write", although the desired effect is probably a different quality of the [r] rather than the absence of [w], since also in Received Pronunciation no sound corresponds to [w] in that word) or replaced by [v] as in "vat" instead of "what", and the difficulty in pronouncing words beginning with vowels, which are made more manageable by adding [y].[46] Commenting on the first conversation, Mendis (1998) points out the inconsistencies – "wife" and "vife", "wanted" and "vill" – which might be an attempt "to indicate the speakers' misconception of the correct distribution of the phonemes" (1998, 66) or – I would add – might have been intentionally introduced by the author to warn the reader against taking these peculiarities at face value and believing them to be distinctive traits always characterizing Tamil speakers of English.

Sinhalese speakers of English, instead, are characterized by the use of Sinhala interjections and a structuring of sentences based on the process of relexification mentioned in Chapter Three. As there are no

---

[46] As Prof. Siromi Fernando of the University of Colombo pointed out, it is a difficulty shared by Sri Lankan Tamils and Indians, who adjust the pronunciation to their system through the anteposition of the consonant [y].

fully developed Sinhalese characters, the following is possibly the only dialogue, or one of the few, between native speakers of Sinhala, while usually one of the two parties is a Burgher, as the second example will show:

> "Adai," hissed one, "you saw? Nobody in the engine."
> "Can't be," said the other, "somewhere must be."
> "So where? Look, will you, if inside."
> A moment later: "Adai, a good thing I'll tell?"
> "What?"
> "Put the body on the engine front."
> "Can't, can't. How? Will fall off."
> "How if tie up? I'll some rope bring." (*YY*, 67)

> "For tomorrow morning breakfast you make hoppers, you heard? [...] Don't give me some watery muck, did you hear?"
> "*Aiyo*, you're talking as if hopeless curry giving. Master go and wash and change and all. I'll this in the ice box put and early morning cook. Tea, or what you now want? (*YY*, 103)

Gliding over the "master", which is likely to be an exaggeration meant to show the false subservience of the cook, both examples show untranslated words, *adai*, "a slang term which can function both as a term of address and as a way of getting somebody's attention" (Mendis 1998, 67) and *aiyo*, a Sinhala expression used "loosely in conversation to express pain, dismay, loss or grief" (*JFT*, 9). The two examples metonymically represent Muller's use of Sinhala and Tamil terms, which at times demand an interpretative effort of the reader as in "What the hell are these eekel brooms for? (*YY*, 38), or in "Oi. What's the hoo-ha?" (*YY*, 41), but more often are glossed in parentheses or explained in footnotes, thus creating explicit instances of authorial intrusiveness. While the use of local terms belongs to a kind of ethnographic writing meant to constitute new experiences and new places, it also "signifies the self-conscious processes of language variation in which the text is engaged" (Ashcroft *et al.* 1989, 56-57); difference is thus selectively made more or less evident on the written page (through italics, parenthetical glossing, untranslated words) and, although inversely proportional in linguistic terms, the relationship between English and Sinhala/Tamil in the texts seems to symbolize the Burghers' position in Sri Lanka – sparsely present, however constitutive of the overall fabric, and mainly requiring a bridge (be it translation or cultural adaptation) to relate to their surroundings.

From a syntactic point of view, the most remarkable aspects in the conversations quoted above, however, concern the lack of subject and object pronouns and the end position of verbs. The former, which carries negative associations of lack of education and prestige, is often found in the so-called basilectal variety of Sri Lankan English (Fernando, 1989; 1990), probably as a kind of simplification based on the fact that Sinhala is a pro-drop language that often elides pronouns and the verb "be" and relies on Gricean conversational principles whereby the addressee of a message will be able to infer the missing links (Kandiah, 1981; 1990). The latter is the result of the superimposition of English lexis on the pattern of Sinhala, which, as Mendis (1998) states, is an SOV language that in its colloquial variety requires the fronting of "somewhere" or other place adverbials. If it is true that the speech acts thus reproduced are biased in that they do not portray the Sinhalese as educated speakers of English, it is just as true that their sentences are credible because they are formulated according to a system that finds widespread usage and that has in fact strongly influenced the formation of that disputed variety known as Sri Lankan English.[47] In fairness to Muller, it must be said that linguistic mockery and stereotyping are not limited to the Sinhalese and the Tamils. In fact, apart from the narrator, whose English, however distinctive, mainly follows standard patterns, the Burghers in the

---

[47] Chapter 3.1 reported that the existence of Sri Lankan English is denied by Fonseka and other scholars.

novels speak a substandard variety where pronouns are often elided, the gerund form –ing is almost regularly used without the auxiliary "be", and tag questions are replaced by the universal "no",[48] as the following examples – boys discussing the events of the Second World War and mourners worrying at a troublesome burial – show:

> "Anyway, these fellows drinking gin an' talking. Ipseems Monty is very angry that fellows in France are saying that Allied tanks are hopeless not like the Germans."
> "Let him be, men, what else were they saying?"
> "Couldn't hear much, men. Said that five Shermans not enough to knock one Panther and our tanks burning all over. One shot from Germans enough."
> "Gwan! All bloody rubbish. If burning like that how everyday they are advancing. Going to Rome also."
> "How do I know? Only telling what I heard, no?"
> (*OUTT*, 94)

> "Someone screaming from inside grave."
> "What? Inside grave?"
> "That's what. Must have buried alive, no?" (*JFT*, 79)

Language is also thematized and intertwined with history, thus forming one of the most important fields where nationalist battles are fought. Despite the light tone of the narrative and the basically apolitical nature of the Burghers in the trilogy, history often figures in explicit digressions through which the chronicler explains events in Ceylon's past, usually taking a critical stance toward the cynicism of the European colonizers, their racial theories, the commercial exploitation they pursued. Thus, there are a number of instances where sarcasm mixes with historical record:

---

[48] See Chapter 3.1.

> The British who came in singing "Rule Britannia" were appalled. Also, they found the central kingdom of Kandy thumbing a nose at Europe in general and blithely carrying on as in the days of yore [...] (*OUTT*, 12)
>
> The British had this monstrous idea that they were actually doing the natives a favour. *Behold! We have descended from our cloud realm to show you how to eat peas.* [...] It was easy to see how the people of Ceylon quickly became not only a subject race, but also quite an abject race. (*OUTT*, 25)
>
> The British had, in a fit of rare humour, named their engines mostly after governors and other colonial big brass. [...] Thus did Sir Andrew Mackenzie race upcountry; Sir William Horton to the south; Sir Frederick North to the north. (*YY*, 9)

Contemporary history, instead, is woven into the text as it impinges on the lives of the Von Blosses. The reader "hears" through their conversations or reflections that the cost of living was very affordable in Ceylon in the 30s; that the Second World War was discussed with curiosity by the Burghers but did not really change living conditions on the island; that the Japanese bombing of Colombo had no real consequence, much as in Ondaatje's *Running in the Family* it is reduced to a misspelling in a telegram.[49] But rising nationalism did worry the Burghers and brought about exclusionary language policies and the taking over of working positions by the Sinhalese, so that many disillusioned Burghers set off on their diaspora to Australia and Canada. In *Yakada Yakā*, the years immediately prior to independence witness a "process of Ceylonization" (186) decreed by the Legislative

---

[49] "[Lalla] received a telegram [...] which read: 'Rain over Colombo', so she put her money on another horse. Dickman Delight galloped to victory on dry turf. Japanese planes had attacked Galle Face Green in Colombo and the telegram should have read: 'Raid over Colombo'. Dickman Delight never won again." (*RF*, 50). The episode is an ironic musing on how history can be rewritten – or even erased – and produce quite different consequences.

Council whereby positions of responsibility have to be handed over to the Sinhalese: in the specific area the book covers, the railways, an example is provided by the apparently trivial exchange between a Tamil stationmaster and the new Sinhalese engine driver who replaces Sonnaboy von Bloss.

> "How, how, brother, you're new driver? Vayair is that von Bloss man?
> Stembo studied Sinnathamby. "Colombo. Transferred. Why?"
> "Addadda! Vain he vent. Vaiting to give him. Cumming here and telling how I mus' vair youniform in my station. Vart, brother, this is north, no?
> "So?"
> [...]
> Stembo gave a sharp hoot, leaned out, studied Sinnathamby. "Rules," he said. "No nonsense. Wear cap. I am Sinhalese. Not like von Bloss. This is my country." (*YY*, 201)

The dialogue might seem a simplification of the attitudes of the time, but, even granting a degree of stereotyping, it does reveal the impending tensions deriving from the Tamils' feeling that the north had its own customs and regulations, and the angry re-appropriation of the country by the Sinhalese.

Somewhat patronizingly, Muller writes:

> The great Sinhala urge had begun. Sinhalese children flocked the hall of Academia and wrestled with the niceties of the English tongue. [...] The frenzied attempts to grapple with and conquer English was, in the beginning, both pathetic and hilarious.
> [...]

> With learning, they came to realize that this was their country and what the blazes were the British doing here anyway?
>
> A new nationalism began to raise its head – a nationalism that ganged the Sinhalese together. They had a cause: their land. (*YY*, 113-14)

English education was at this stage still highly desirable as it obviously provided the key to enter the Civil Service and occupy the managing positions hitherto reserved to the British or to top-class Burghers. Sarvan (2001) very aptly notices how the condescending tone of the chronicler, who laughed at the difficulties met by Sinhalese students of English, is redeemed shortly after by an episode in which a Sinhalese uses the word "altercation" and the Burgher engine driver does not understand it: "You're a Burgher and you don't know English?" (*YY*, 217). Commenting on the handover of power, Sarvan asks: "Why were the Burghers not ready to occupy these posts? Why did they lack the desire?" (2001, 530). It is a point worth considering, as it problematizes the univocal value of Sinhalese nationalism. It is however a fact that the latter gained more and more power and promoted an increasingly essentialist identity that rejected the pluralism of the past. In this sense, the imposition of Sinhala as the only language was an act of betrayal toward minorities and created, in even sharper tones, an internal hierarchical and exclusionary system analogous to the colonial one. Fictionally, this appears when Sonnaboy, now an experienced driver, has to "pass [a] qualifying exam in Sinhala" (*YY*, 228):

> "So I asked the Divisional Inspector what do I want Sinhala for to drive an engine? All the bloody engines and diesels coming from England and Germany and Canada, no? What? These are Sinhalese engines? Must talk to them in Sinhala?" (*ibid.*)

And later on, to the incredulity of the Burghers, things get worse:

> "And now saying will not teach English any more in the schools. Children must do all the subjects in Sinhala. Hell of a joke, no?"
>
> To Bunty de Kretser he said: "What about our bloody mother tongue? Our mother tongue is English, no? Who is talking Sinhala in our homes?" (*ibid.*)

The *kaduwa* of English was thus being brandished against those people that seemed to embody the former colonial masters. So, while the Tamils developed their own forms of resistance, the Burghers felt that, just as in 1796 the British takeover of Ceylon had given them the choice to "stay and be ruled or go to Indonesia" (*OUTT*, 217), the new political situation put them in the same position:

> It took just eight years, eight years after Independence, for the cosy world of Sri Lanka's Burghers to collapse. Once again the choice: adapt or leave . . . and most left. (*OUTT*, 219)

The community shrank dramatically and, as the chronicler reports, in 1991 the Burghers amounted to a mere 0.8% of the population. But their resilience and the slight softening of nationalistic policies have helped them to overcome the crisis:

> They may still be, in the main, the "eat, drink and be merry" men of their particular Sherwood Forest, but they are all Sinhala-educated today, mix with enthusiasm, intermarry with almost boisterous abandon and remain an object lesson of how a tiny minority can live in absolute freedom and security. (*JFT*, 137).

4.2.2 *Colombo: A Novel:* **Deconstructing the City**

Colombo: A Novel (1995), the subtitle a necessary label the publisher wanted to have on the cover, said the author, marks an even greater departure from a kind of nostalgic "village writing" that characterized much Sri Lankan literature in English. If the Burgher trilogy was mainly set in urban areas, Colombo, as the title anticipates, provides a multi-faceted image of Sri Lanka's capital whose spaces and places allow Muller to engage with a number of historical and social issues. Bricolage and intertextuality play a relevant role in this substantial collation of official chronicles, personal memories, news items, fictional passages and social criticism, which, mainly linked through a constant interaction of present and past, colonial and indigenous exploitation, condemnation and nostalgia, would justify the coining of the term "bookumentary" to denote an exploratory tour the narrator leads the reader on, during which past and present are constantly juxtaposed – at times revealing analogies in history, at other times jarring contrasts – thus shedding light on some of the least known aspects of the city, and considering both its evolution and today's corollary of corruption and conflict.

Whether because of the eagerness to voice his discontent or by consciously adopting a postmodern stance, Muller seems to have espoused Thomas Docherty's "economy of difference", that is, the idea that "representation is no longer conceivable as a simple 'duplication' or substitutive mimetic doubling: representation is now 'excessive' or economically dysfunctional" (1996, 64), which makes of *Colombo* a quasi-picaresque text where every "station" prompts musings, memories, quotations or the recording of events that either match precisely or contrast stridently the specific portion of cityscape. Muller himself acknowledges that

> the episodal contents of this book have been narrated in support of the specific themes contained, and are based on real-term approximations to the typical city scenario of

Colombo's nights. These are penned to draw attention primarily to the immensity of the many problems that would beset any crowded Asian city. (ix)

Narrative unifying principles are disrupted: there is no unifying plot nor recurring characters except the narrator, so that it is difficult to delineate a general pattern for the twenty-seven self-contained chapters which, in their almost casual juxtaposition, can be read as a metaphor for the sprawling city defying the order that the Europeans tried to introduce. It is possible, however, to notice how Colombo's topography starts from the Fort, the stronghold of power around which the city spreads, moves then to its adjacent areas with occasional forays to peripheral districts, to go back in the second, brief, part of the book to the Fort and its immediate surroundings, retracing in a more systematic way the succession of events that shaped its history. A certain degree of coherence is also traceable in structural repetition: in spite of the very heterogeneous material, many chapters are introduced by a description of an area, a historical reconstruction or considerations about an aspect of city life, followed by an episode which, mostly appalling or cruel, is meant to illustrate and substantiate a thesis.

Sri Lanka's capital city features as the main – actually the only – character. Avoiding the usual cartographic pretence of finiteness – whereby the portion of world shown is seen as circumscribed and detached from its surroundings – the map taking shape through the narrator and the reader's wanderings is thus not just a background against which characters move according to a plot, but rather a tentacular body stretching in many directions and ensnaring humans – little more than paradigmatic examples – who seem to be moved by the crude laws of determinism rather than by their own volition. And the knowing narrator, who however relies heavily on the most disparate sources, seems engaged in a reworking on a small scale of the literary paradigms of the travel narrative and the quest narrative, where the latter prevails with its attempt at revealing truths that mere descriptions would glide over.

Colombo is dissected along the two axes of time and space, with the former further subdivided into past and present and the latter looked at in both its institutional or standard functions and its human aspects. This kind of analysis and the sprawling images that result accumulate details that portray space as it is conceived – the ideas attached to it, its memories, the connotations it evokes – as it is perceived, that is, how it is empirically definable, and as it is lived in its human and social dimension. This inclusive approach reminds of Foucault's concept of heterotopia, that is, the product of our cultural ability to simultaneously construct a place as a real, an imagined and an inhabited space. Thus, for example, the orientalist projections of exoticized and eroticized landscapes duly purified of any reference to unpalatable aspects which are deployed in the persuading discourse of guides and tourist brochures are deflated by an almost constant exposure of what lies below the surface, be it children sold into slavery, prostitution or the beggars' racket.

Muller seems to assume the position that John Douthwaite (1998), quoting I.G. Cook, identifies as that of radical geographers, who postulate a strict determinism whereby the development of individual conscience is shaped by collective socio-economic and historical processes; thus, "The Canalians" for example, highlights the analogy between water "moving morosely", where "everything that people discard with a twinge of shame – shame in what they shed – finds a grave", where "fish have white fungus around their gills and the brew is syrup-thick at times, bloated with poison" (*C,* 64), and the equally rotting people who live there, "the drifters, the derelicts, the overflowing chaff of the interior and the riff-raff of the city" (65). Within the same description, however, the narrator goes back to the time when the canals were built and, in one of the many instances of intertextuality, refers to R. L. Brohier's *Links between Sri Lanka and the Netherlands: A Book of Dutch Ceylon*, quoting its "fascinating waterspreads" that "contributed [...] to the splendid prosperity of the district they served" (*ibid.*).

Abandoning linear representation and traditional cartographic practices, the construction of Colombo is obtained through a rhizomatic map that develops by putting the narrator on the same axis as the reader, so that they are perceived to be walking together along its streets: "It is no more than a mile from Slave Island to the Fort" (10), "We cross this and the pavement dazzles" (27), "But walk this same Main Street with me today" (26), with the narrator providing information about landmarks, beauties and eyesores: "Main Street – main thoroughfare of the 'inner citadel' of the Dutch." (26), "Here then, was an emporium" (31), "in Mutwal, just before the point where the road turns past the dockyard into St James Street" (97), and at times parodying promotional formulae belied by the unattractive features shown: "Come to Colombo. You can almost persuade yourself that you are witnessing a procession of tramps [...] See them at sundown." (24).

To further illustrate how space and time (and occasionally language) interact, I will quote a few more examples. Differently from most chapters, which open with a geographical or historical description, the first is introduced by a brief atmospheric passage portraying sunset on the seashore followed by a fictional episode which immediately highlights recurring themes such as sexual harassment, shabby lives, the worsening conditions of life in the city. Sitting under an umbrella in an attempt to enjoy a shadow of intimacy, a young woman and her boyfriend respectively experience the frustration of being made the object of lewd attention and not having a car or a decent home to retreat to. After seeing the vicious passers-by through her eyes, the perspective changes:

> Trapped. Trapped in this large public esplanade where once long ago, the bastion of St Jeronimo would have glowered at them from the fortress of Colombo. (4)

While creating a link between the outside world and the girl's emotions, the adjective that opens the paragraph – dramatic in effect as its past participle form hints at the result of a process of entrapment at many levels – takes the reader into the physical environment of the novel, the city of Colombo, and establishes the relationship between the two coordinates of space and time which will inform the narration. Time eludes both cyclical and linear movement, shifting from a "now" of the narration to a "then" to be more precisely identified in past history, to the non-time of most fictional passages, which seem frozen in a bubble; space and time interact, the one prompting glimpses of the other, in a relation which reminds of the Indian iconography depicting "time as a coiled serpent, the *Ananta*, who forms the seat or bed of Vishnu, the supporter of space." (Devy 1998, 80). "Trapped", then, expresses her feelings, but also metaphorically the position of the town, whose first two named features are clearly identifiable as belonging to a military colonial past. The parallelism is brought on in the next paragraph, where Colombo, just like the two lovers, is "disguising itself in a gathering gloom." A detailed description follows, indicating those actual landmarks which allow to locate the set of the action on a map:

> To their left, as they sat, the Galle Face Hotel – a chocolate gateaux of amber lights and frosted fluorescence. Behind them, contemplating their umbrella tent, the tall statue of S. W. R. D. Bandaranaike. [. . .] This was the Galle Face Green – a big dust-skirted lung in a city of smoking buses and melting tar on hot roads and clogged, festering drains and whores outside the Hilton and the Inter-Continental and at the top of Baillie Street. (4)

The setting is thus contained between the sunset on the sea, the fortress on the right, the hotel on the left and the statue behind. Again, the choice to show the characters surrounded by those landmarks which define and circumscribe their world could be read as symbolical of Colombo's (or Sri Lanka's) condition: from the open sea came the European invaders who left their mark on the territory in the form of fortifications and great colonial hotels still visible to this day, to be handed over in the post-independence era to local politicians, whose first great representative, shot dead on his doorstep in 1959, is however a controversial figure as many consider him responsible for exacerbating the divide between Sinhalese and Tamils. Hence a multi-layered reading hinting at the trapped condition of a city/country subjected to centuries of foreign domination with their aftermath of socio-political turmoil and ethnic division, which the characters come to embody through not too explicit but still recognizable devices such as their names – the Sinhalese Kusum and the (probably) Tamil Anton – and the information about their family backgrounds. The static quality of this parody of a postcard finds its linguistic equivalence in the lack of verbs of action. In fact, apart from the couple, who however are sitting, every element is described through the indefiniteness of gerunds and participles in a growing sense of paralysis. Muller seems to be operating a camera, in a slow pan that zooms in on and freezes certain scenes, so that people and things are caught in motion, yet shown as still.

After a flashback through which the noise of the traffic evokes the battles fought on the Green in the past, the narrating voice becomes very matter-of-fact:

> Colombo. The capital. Seat of government; of commerce. It was capital to the British and the administrative seat of the Portuguese and Dutch. On the map it lies 7°N, 79°48'E. The British guarded it with some three hundred pieces of heavy cannon. Its Fort rang to the drunken revelry of the Dutch. It was fed by slaves and rose on the black backs and shoulders of the natives. (7)

The detached information summarizing the historical and geographical facts that define the city gives way to bitter considerations about the exploitation and the military force that the colonial powers exercised. The passage provides a bridge to the next fictional move as well as to the subsequent freezeframe on a near area of town:

> Anton walked slowly to his little room in Slave Island. [...] He always quickened his steps across the railway to plunge into the crowded pavements of Slave Island. Men with gaudy sarongs, raised and knotted at the crotch, women in Bata sandals and slippers, the Petromax lights of glass-fronted carts selling breadfruit chips and bondi and jellabies.
>
> [...]
>
> Three hundred years ago, Slave Island was a rugged peninsula, joined by causeway and bridges to the Fort of Colombo. It divided the lake, which narrowed into a moat and was linked to the old, winding sally port and Point de Galle which is the Galle Buck of today.
> There are no slaves today – or are there? (7)

The fictional character becomes a ferryman taking the reader across the arm of the Beira Lake that separates the seafront from Slave Island, a modern-day inferno whose door is announced by the squabble of black bats in a tree by the level crossing. The description of the crowd hints at the current invasions from the West: the Petromax lanterns lighting sarongs and Bata shoes provide a glimpse of how traditional customs recede where big multinationals spread, while the presence of this image in relation to reflections on slavery might be read as pointing towards a critique of those agents of globalization that not only fuel the logic of the market by creating new needs and imposing models and products from elsewhere, but also thrive on outsourcing, that is, using underpaid labour in developing countries. Differently from other names given by the colonizers, Slave

Island might have officially lost its literal meaning, but the link between signifier and referent – broken by the law that abolished slavery back in 1844 – *de facto* still exists.

The import of names is further developed in the second chapter, where the narrator explains how the capital's name – Kolon Tota for the Sinhalese, Kollam for the Tamils and Kolamba in Sanskrit – was made sense of by the Europeans by linking the phonetic resemblance of the local name with a word they could identify as meaningful. The Sanskrit name, which according to popular claim derives from *kola-amba*, a species of particularly leafy but fruitless mango tree, was reproduced as Columbum by the Papal legate arriving there in 1347 (237), and definitely consolidated three centuries later, when the Dutch created a coat-of-arms for the city featuring a tree and a dove, thereby linking the native word with the almost homophonous Latin term *columba*. Thus doubled, the name arouses bitter considerations on the reality it stands for: "A leafy mango tree. No fruit. Only a poison milk from every broken branch!" (22), while it is interesting to notice how the Dutch, who added a traditional symbol of peace, were deploying military force, torture and slavery in their governance of the island.

The false promise of names is further emphasized in the chapter devoted to the Pettah, the "old town" of the Dutch, renamed by the British with an "Anglo-Indian term derived from the Tamil *Pettai*, which was the name given in India for the suburb of a fort" (20). It is today the biggest market area in town, loud, run-down and chaotic, a place of which it is said:

> All the fakes and imitations of the Orient are here. Seiko watches without the 'e', Canon cameras with a double 'n', goods made in 'Enland', not England, and those fripperies [...] that come out of Taiwan and Thailand." (27)

In his scathing observation, the narrator highlights a corruption of the relationship linking the sign to its referent, which is and is not the object promised. There seems to be a "Third Orient" imitating the "First Orient", and both in turn imitate products and symbols of a lifestyle introduced by the West. Interestingly, Muller opts for the more literary and connoted term, the one that has long been debated as carrier of a projected exotic attitude, thus ironically reversing the *topos* of fabled treasures awaiting their finders. It is, however, also an expression of contempt which might derive from his own otherness and, to a certain degree, "Europeanness" in the Sri Lankan context. The description also provides a concrete, however trivial, instance of that sense of worthlessness which has often been seen as part of the heritage of a colonial past, the loss of awareness and pride in local culture and artefacts and the correlated need to receive approval or recognition from those who have proved to be superior. The counterfeited "Enland" finds an echo in "this other England" (460), a phrase summarizing the physical and institutional system so thoroughly applied to the island that "there wasn't, by the turn of the century, any way in which the citizen of Colombo could escape the stamp of the Britisher" (460). That stamp, then as today, is but an imperfect copy and could thus be read as a mockery of the assumed superiority, a way in which the "natives" appropriate a traditional sign of guarantee.

The Dutch canal in Wellawatte becomes the setting where a ghost-like mother pulls a makeshift cart with her lymphademic baby to reach her usual begging spot in Galle Road, where she joins other crippled and deformed beggars. Concluding the paragraph, the narrating voice comments:

> It was time to set up the exhibition.
>
> Are people here of the mendicant or begging races?
> William Maxwell Wood, who was a surgeon [...] thought the latter. [...] he recorded how the Cingalese (Sinhalese) '. . . if he has nothing in the shape of trade by which to rob the passing stranger, he still thinks he has the right of

contribution, and if you glance at him on the wayside, out comes his soliciting hand with a salaam; and smirking fathers will hold forth the hand of the infant in arms, to beg of the passer-by.'

[...]

Even Edward Lear [...] saw the beggars, called them 'odious' and declared that they 'bully one out of all patience'.
(44)

While the immediate impression is that the voices are reported in order to expose judgemental and racist attitudes, one cannot but be disturbed by the narrator's words: "Here, beggars are not just the victims of social collapse. They are the products of an assembly line. They are manufactured!" (45), followed by two illustrative fictional passages. The gaze upon the beggars comes from a privileged position and reveals both a criticism not dissimilar from that of the Westerners and the expression of a cultural divide that echoes the "them" and "us" of colonial times.

A similar cynicism is shown in the chapter "Let Sleeping Gods Lie", where the island's religions are ironically described:

> The Buddha sleeps best, since he has been perpetuated in a reclining posture in many Colombo temples and image houses. [...] Sleep claims him in other temples, and scholars have even come to identify the position of the knees to determine whether it is sleep or simply relaxation.
>
> Allah the Merciful sleeps, but fitfully. He is assailed at the oddest night hours by his faithful who proclaim him great and remind him to shower them with wealth.
>
> [...]
>
> The Bhagavan of the Hindus has a good night's sleep. So many other godlets and goddesses and semi-gods and half-

> gods remain on duty and have become so popular that he, the life-giver, has nothing of great merit to concern himself with.
> [...]
> Jesus Christ sleeps on his cross. He learnt the trick after being forced to hang on it for almost two thousand years. The Christians never allowed him to come down from it.
> [...]
> The devils, of course, are wide awake. (76-77)

While alluding to the shortcomings of each religion, which in its sleeping condition seems unable to contrast disgregating forces within the community, this irreverent, rather grotesque review concludes with a consideration of how "People wear their faith with [...] much ceremony. [...] It is worn with pride, noted by others also in their distinctive attire, then carefully hung away until the next time out" (78). The critique seems aimed mostly at the Sinhalese who, when the Dutch demanded religious membership as a necessary requisite to obtain state employment, "conformed quite cynically and practised their own religion in private" (93), while the prouder Portuguese Catholics preferred to leave the capital. In a flashback, we learn how, confiding that their gods would protect them against waves of invading Europeans, the people of Kandy were finally defeated by the British. The conquest carried out by the "white invaders with their clerics who were even better organized and more intent than the soldiers" (84) ebbed after independence, when Buddhism was revived and inscribed within a broader nationalistic discourse leading to intolerance. Sarcastically, the chronicler reports that many temples have now been commodified as tourist attractions, with innumerable Bo trees sold as the original tree that witnessed the Buddha's enlightenment, and goes further by claiming that

> Colombo's many places of worship command prime locations on the richest, most attractive tracts of land [...] A massive mosque rises behind the Town Hall; the Vajiramya

Buddhist temple lies in the heart of Colombo Four; St. Lucia's Cathedral stands stately in Kotahena [...]." (91)

Once again, criticism reaches the past and the present, imported and local evils.

An aspect which cannot go unnoticed is the abundance of sex crimes and abuse in the fictional passages. Sex is abundantly present in the Burgher trilogy, where extremely sensitive family episodes related to incest, rape and homosexuality are exposed in farcical tones probably meant to exorcize the author's own experiences. His treatment of sexuality takes a different colour in *Colombo*, where it is portrayed as dark, traumatic and often relying on a net of illicit family or social connivance so as to stress its most despicable and poisonous aspects. While most of it might well be reflecting reality, one cannot but perceive echoes of de Quincey's erotic feminization of Sri Lanka:

> She is hot; she is cold. She is civilized; she is barbarous. [...] She has all the climates; she is the 'Pandora of Islands', all-gifted and ready, if approached properly, to give everything. Ceylon will but too deeply fulfil the functions of a paradise. Too subtly she will lay fascinations upon man. (Silva 2004a, 124)

Allegedly, it is the fairly conventional image of sensuousness attached to the oriental island that corrupts man. Anger and disgust are often palpable in a wording which, in its all-out attack against past and present evils, past and present rulers, occasionally reveals a tinge of nostalgia for the good old days and a certain contempt of the Sinhalese, an aspect that casts some doubt on the more compassionate comments in other parts of the book. Muller might thus be resorting to an almost contemptuous European stance that in the indulging and amoral "natives" sees a metonymy of the island – a reaction to a country that for all its pluralism in race, religion and culture, still promotes the myth of an essential identity based on racial purity and relegates the Burgher to a condition of in-betweenness.

Conclusions

The images depicted by Ondaatje's and Muller's novels question, in different ways, established identities and conventional constructions of geography, history and language. Geography is interrogated in its theoretical assumptions by Ondaatje, while Muller looks at it as an identity marker in the trilogy and becomes a postmodern map-maker intent on deconstructing the city in *Colombo*. Without really engaging directly in a confrontation with colonialism, both refer to its legacy and to the way it contributed to the shaping of Sri Lankan identities, while the broader field of historical knowledge is explored in ways that refrain from univocality and privilege instead plural voices, individual memory and rumour, thereby giving fictional renderings to the findings of the Subaltern Studies Group. Language and translation are both reflected upon and used in ways that draw attention to the ideological operations that can be performed through them and to the ways they participate in the shaping of realities and identities. What emerges in both authors is an emphasis on language being used as an instrument of power and empire, but at the same time as an expression of heart and community. Finally, while Ondaatje abstains from defining identity, preferring to postulate it as positional and shifting, Muller seems to confirm the fixity of stereotypes, but by so doing in fact subverts many of the conventional traits ascribed to the Burghers.

The analyses and interpretations emerging from the perusal (in its broadest meaning referred to in Chapter One) of Ondaatje's and Muller's texts are the result of a journey that has led me to explore the territories of geography, history and translation, the assumptions and conventions that inform their discourses and, above all, the way in which their constructs influence the shaping of identities. Post-structuralism, deconstruction and post-colonial studies have provided the background for an investigation that, far from being exhaustive, has however tried to ground itself in the specificity of Sri Lankan culture. Being aware that geographical and cultural distance requires greater care of approach in order to avoid simplifications and stereotyping, I have tried to contextualize my analysis by including information about various aspects of the country, especially in relation to the projections of exclusionary identities upon which the rhetoric of the civil war was based.

I am aware that the texts analyzed lend themselves to readings that could highlight other motifs pertaining, for example, to aspects of performance and theatricality in the Burgher lifestyle as portrayed by both authors, to their ample recourse to intertextuality, to issues of gender and race. Also, the tensions deriving from the socio-political situation and the civil war could be further investigated in Muller's *Children of the Lion* (1997), a rewriting of the myths and legends on which the Sinhalese foundational chronicles are based, and in some of the short stories contained in *All God's Children* (2004), with their ghastly exposure of terror and military training camps. Moreover, identity, war and trauma also figure in the novels and poems of authors like Jean Arasanayagam, Shyam Selvadurai, Nihal de Silva and Anne Ranasinghe and a study of their literary production would certainly enrich the perspective. Bearing all this in mind, I cannot but hope that this small contribution will be complemented by other lines of investigation of Sri Lankan literature in English.

Bibliography

Adam, Ian, and Helen Tiffin. *Past the Last Post: Theorizing Post-colonialism and Post-modernism*. Hemel Hempstead: Harvester Wheatsheaf, 1991.

Adejunmobi, Moradewun. "African Writing and European Languages." *Translator* 4, no. 2 (1998): 163-180.

Albertazzi, Silvia. *Lo sguardo dell'altro*. Roma: Carocci, 2000.

Anderson, Benedict. *Imagined Communities: Reflections on the Origin and Spread of Nationalism*. London: Verso, 1983.

Arasanayagam, Jean. *Apocalypse '83*. Colombo: ICES, 2003.

Arasaratnam, Sinappah. *Ceylon*. Englewood Cliff, New Jersey: Prentice Hall, 1964.

Ashcroft, Bill, Gareth Griffiths, and Helen Tiffin. *The Empire Writes Back: Theory and Practice in Post-colonial Literatures*. London: Routledge, 1989.

___, eds. *The Post-colonial Studies Reader*. London: Routledge, 1995.

Attridge, Derek, Geoff Bennington, and Robert Young, eds. *Poststructuralism and the Question of History*. Cambridge: Cambridge University Press, 1987.

Awasthy, Rajendra, ed. *Selected Tamil Short Stories*. New Delhi: Fusion Books, 2004.

Baker, Mona, ed. *Routledge Encyclopaedia of Translation Studies*. London: Routledge, 1988.

Bassnett-McGuire, Susan. *Comparative Literature: A Critical Introduction*. Oxford: Blackwell, 1993.

___. *Translation Studies*. London: Routledge, 1991.

Bassnett, Susan, and Harish Trivedi, eds. *Postcolonial Translation: Theory and Practice*. London: Routledge, 1999.

Bassnett, Susan, and Harish Trivedi. "Introduction: Of Colonies, Cannibals and Vernaculars." In *Postcolonial Translation: Theory and Practice*, ed. Bassnett and Trivedi, 1-18. London: Routledge, 1999.

Berman, Antoine, trans. *The Experience of the Foreign: Culture and Translation in Romantic Germany.* Albany: State University of New York Press, 1992.
Betts, Raymond F. *Decolonization.* London: Routledge, 1998.
Bhabha, Homi. *The Location of Culture.* New York: Routledge, 1994.
Boehmer, Elleke. *Colonial & Postcolonial Literature.* Oxford: Oxford U.P., 1995.
Brennan, Timothy. "The National Longing for Form." In *The Post-colonial Studies Reader*, ed. Ashcroft, Griffiths and Tiffin, 170-175. London: Routledge, 1995.
Canagarajah, Suresh A. "Competing Discourses in Sri Lankan English Poetry." *World Englishes* 13, no. 3 (1994): 361-376.
___. "The Politics of Code Choice: Bilingualism in the 'Liberated Zone.'" *Navasilu* 15 & 16 (1998): 11-18.
Canary, Robert H., and Henry Kozicki, eds. *The Writing of History: Literary Form and Historical Understanding.* Madison: The University of Wisconsin Press, 1978.
Chakrabarty, Dipesh. "Postcoloniality and the Artifice of History." In *The Post-colonial Studies Reader*, ed. Ashcroft, Griffiths and Tiffin, 383-388. London: Routledge: 1995.
Chamberlain, Lory. "Gender and the Metaphorics of Translation." In *Rethinking Translation: Discourse, Subjectivity, Ideology*, ed. Venuti, 57-74. London: Routledge, 1992.
Chambers, Iain. *Paesaggi migratori: Cultura e identità nell'epoca postcoloniale.* Genova: Costa & Nolan, 1996.
Chambers, Iain, and Lidia Curti. *La questione postcoloniale.* Napoli: Liguori, 1997.
Chatterjee, Partha. *The Nation and its Fragments: Colonial and Postcolonial Histories.* Princeton: Princeton U.P., 1993.
Clifford, James. *The Predicament of Culture.* Cambridge, MA: Harvard U.P., 1988.
Coetzee, John M. *Dusklands.* Johannesburg: Raven Press, 1974.

___. *White Writing: On the Culture of Letters in South Africa.* New Haven: Yale U.P., 1988.

Comaroff, Jean, and John. "Criminal Obsessions, after Foucault, Postcoloniality, Policing, and the Metaphysics of Disorder." *Critical Enquiry* 30, no. 4 (2004): 800-824.

Comellini, Carla. "Geography and History as Literary Themes and Devices at Work in Michael Ondaatje's *The English Patient.*" In *Routes of the Roots: Geography and Literature in the English-Speaking Countries*, ed. Zoppi, 345-354. Roma: Bulzoni, 1998.

Concilio, Carmen. "The City as Text(ure): Bombay in Salman Rushdie's *The Ground Beneath Her Feet.*" In *The Great Work of Making Real. Salman Rushdie's* The Ground Beneath Her Feet, ed. Linguanti and Tchernichova, 129-149. Pisa: ETS, 2003.

Conrad, Joseph. "Geography and Some Explorers." 1926. In *Tales of Hearsay / Last Essays.* Reprint, London: Routledge / Thoemmes Press, 1995.

Cook, Rufus. "'Imploding Time and Geography': Narrative Compressions in Michael Ondaatje's *The English Patient.*" *Journal of Commonwealth Literature* 33, 2 (1998): 109-125.

Coughlan, Peter. "Meander, If You Want to Get to Town. A Conversation with Michael Ondaatje." http://www.kiriyamaprize.org/winners/2000/2000ondaat_interview.shtml.

Cronin, Michael. "Translation and Minority Languages in a Global Age." *Translator* 4, no. 2 (1998): 145-162.

Curran, Beverley. "Ondaatje's *The English Patient* and Altered States of Narrative." *CLCWeb: Comparative Literature and Culture* 6, 3 (2004). http://docs.lib.purdue.edu/clcweb/vol6/iss3/3.

D'haen, Theo, and Hans Bertens, eds. *Liminal Postmodernisms: The Postmodern, the (Post-)Colonial, and the (Post-)Feminist.* Amsterdam: Rodopi, 1994.

De Chickera, Ruwanthie. *Middle of Silence.* Colombo. ICES, 2001.

Derrida, Jacques., trans. *Margins: Of Philosophy.* Brighton: Harvester, 1982.

___, trans. "Des Tours de Babel." In *Difference in Translation*, ed. Graham, 209-248. Ithaca: Cornell U.P., 1985.

De Silva, K. M. *A History of Sri Lanka*. Delhi: Oxford U.P., 1981.

Devy, Ganesh. N. "Time, Territory and Literature." In *Routes of the Roots: Geography and Literature in the English-Speaking Countries*, ed. Zoppi, 73-84. Roma: Bulzoni, 1998.

Disanayaka, J. B. *Understanding the Sinhalese*. Colombo: S. Godage & Bros., 1998.

Docherty, Thomas. *Alterities: Criticism, History, Representation*. Oxford: Clarendon Press, 1996.

Douthwaite, John. "Anomie: Universal Processes and Local Instantiations in Chinua Achebe's *No Longer at Ease*." In *Routes of the Roots: Geography and Literature in the English-Speaking Countries*, ed. Zoppi, 175-212. Roma: Bulzoni, 1998.

Durix, Jean-Pierre. *Mimesis, Genres and Post-colonial Discourse: Deconstructing Magic Realism*. London: Palgrave Macmillan, 1998.

Ewbank, Inga-Stina. "'Open to Encounters': Some Thoughts on Translation as Criticism and Creation." *Kunapipi* XXX, no. 1 (2003): 14-20.

Fanon, Frantz, trans. *Black Skin, White Masks*. New York: Grove Press, 2008.

Fernando, Chitra. "The Nature of Language Inequality: the Case of English and Sinhala from a Functional Point of View." *Navasilu*, 9 (1987): 47-59.

Fernando, Mervyn. *This Piece of Planet Earth Sri Lanka*. Pilyandala: Subodhi, 1999.

Fernando, Siromi. "Speech Situations in Sri Lankan English Fiction: Creating Adequate Style Ranges." *Navasilu* 10 (1990): 107-125.

___. "Style Range in Sri Lankan English Fiction: An Analysis of Four Texts." *World Englishes* 8, no. 2 (1989): 119-131.

___. "The Vocabulary of Sri Lankan English: Words and Phrases That Transform a Foreign Language into Their Own." 9th International Conference on Sri Lanka Studies, Matara, 28th-30th Nov. 2003.

Fonseka, Gamini. "Sri Lankan English: Exploding the Fallacy." 9th International Conference on Sri Lanka Studies, Matara, 28th-30th Nov. 2003.

Fortunati, Vita. "Introduction to Cultural Memory in Geographical Peripheral European Countries." Cultural Memory in Geographical Peripheral European Countries, Malta 7-9 May 2004. http://www2.lingue.unibo.it/acume/agenda/malta/abstracts/Fortunati.htm.

Foucault, Michel, trans. *The Archaeology of Knowledge.* 1972. Reprint, Abingdon, Oxon: Routledge, 2004.

___, trans. *Discipline and Punish: The Birth of the Prison.* New York: Pantheon Books, 1977.

___, trans. "Questions on Geography." In *Power/Knowledge: Selected Interviews and Other Writings 1972-1977*, 63-77. New York: Pantheon, 1980.

Gates, Henry Louis, Jr., ed. *"Race", Writing, and Difference.* Chicago: University of Chicago Press, 1985.

Glover, Brenda. "Unanchored to the World: Displacement and Alienation in *Anil's Ghost* and the Prose of Michael Ondaatje." *CRNLE Journal* (2000): 75-80. http://ehlt.flinders.edu.au/english/CRNLE/CRNLEjournal.html.

Godlewska, Anne, and Neil Smith, eds. *Geography and Empire.* Oxford: Blackwell, 1994.

Gooneratne, Yasmine. "Cultural Independence and the Writer in Sri Lanka." In *Society and the Writer: Essays on Literature in Modern Asia*, ed. Wang Gungwu, David Marr and M. Guerrero, 281-293. Canberra: Australian National U.P., 1981.

___. *Diverse* Inheritance. Adelaide: Centre for Research in the New Literatures in English, 1980.

___. "Introduction." In *Stories from Sri Lanka*, 1-22. Singapore: Heinemann Asia, 1979.

___. "Making History in Sri Lanka: Comic Modes of Satire and Fiction." In *The Writer as Historical Witness: Studies in Commonwealth Literature*, ed. Thumboo and Kandiah, 368-379. Singapore: Unipress, 1995.

Goonetilleke, D. C. R. A. *Sri Lankan English Literature and the Sri Lankan People 1917-2003*. Colombo: Vijitha Yapa Publications, 2005.

Goonetilleke, Ranjan. "The 1971 Insurgency in Sri Lankan Literature in English." In *The Writer as Historical Witness: Studies in Commonwealth Literature*, ed. Thumboo and Kandiah, 380-392. Singapore: Unipress, 1995.

Graham, Joseph F., ed. *Difference in Translation*. Ithaca: Cornell U.P, 1985.

Guneratne, Arjun. "What's in a Name? Aryans and Dravidians in the Making of Sri Lankan Identity." In *The Hybrid Island*, ed. Silva, 20-40. Reprint, Colombo: The Social Scientists' Association, 2004.

Gunesekera, Manique. "Sri Lankan English: Use or Abuse?" *Navasilu* 17 (2000): 40-49.

Gunesekera, Romesh. *Heaven's Edge*. London: Bloomsbury, 2002.

Heber, Reginald, and Mark Antony De Wolfe Howe. *The Poetical Works of Reginald Heber*. Philadelphia: E. H. Butler & Co., 1858.

Hegel, Georg W. F., trans. *The Philosophy of History*. New York: Dover Publications, 1956.

Herat, Manuel. "Speaking and Writing in Lankan English: a study of native and non-native users of English." *liŋ'gwIs tIk* XXVI, no. 1 (2001). http://hss.fullerton.edu/linguistics.

Hilger, Stephanie M. "Ondaatje's *The English Patient* and Rewriting History." *CLCWeb: Comparative Literature and Culture* 6, no. 3 (2004). http://docs.lib.purdue.edu/clcweb/vol6/iss3/13.

Hillger, Annick. "'And this is the world of nomads in any case': *The Odyssey* as Intertext in Michael Ondaatje's *The English Patient*." *Journal of Commonwealth Literature* 33, no. 1 (1998): 23-33.

Hobsbawm, Eric. *The Age of Empire. 1875-1914*. London: Abacus, 1994.

Hoffman, Eva. *Lost in Translation: Life in a New Language*. London: Minerva, 1991.

Hsu, Hsuan. "Post-Nationalism and the Cinematic Apparatus in Minghella's Adaptation of *The English Patient*." *CLCWeb: Comparative Literature and Culture* 6, no. 3 (2004): http://docs.lib.purdue.edu/clcweb/vol6/iss3/5.

Huggan, Graham. "Decolonizing the map: post-colonialism, post-structuralism and the cartographic connection." *Ariel* 20 (1989): 115-131.

___. *Territorial Disputes: Maps and Mapping Strategies in Contemporary Canadian and Australian Fiction*. Toronto: Toronto U.P, 1994.

Hussein, Ameena. *Race: Identity, Caste & Conflict in the South Asian Context*. Colombo: International Centre for Ethnic Studies, 2004.

Hutcheon, Linda. "*Running in the Family:* The Postmodernist Challenge." In *Spider Blues: Essays on Michael Ondaatje*, ed. Solecki, 301-314. Montréal: Véhicule Press, 1985.

Jacobs, Jane M. *Edge of Empire: Postcolonialism and the City*. London: Routledge, 1996.

Jacobs, Johann U. "Allegorical Spaces and Actual Places in Postcolonial Novels." In *Spaces and Crossings: Essays on Literature and Culture in Africa and Beyond*, ed. Rita Wilson and Carlotta von Maltzan, 197-218. Frankfurt: Peter Lang, 2000.

___. "Michael Ondaatje's *The English Patient* (1992) and Postcolonial Impatience." JLS/TLW 13, nos.1-2 (1997): 92-111.

Jacquemond, Richard. "Translation and Cultural Hegemony: The Case of French-Arabic Translation." In *Rethinking Translation:*

Discourse, Subjectivity, Ideology, ed. Venuti, 139-158. London: Routledge 1992.

Jay, Paul. "Memory, Identity and Empire in Michael Ondaatje's *Running in the Family*." Midwest Modern Language Association, November 2003. http://home.comcast.net/~jay.paul/ondaatje.htm.

Jayatilaka, Tissa. "The English-Language Novel of Sri Lanka and the Critical Response to It: an Overview." *Navasilu* 17 (2000): 1-20.

Jayawardena, Kumari. *Nobodies to Somebodies: The Rise of the Colonial Bourgeoisie in Sri Lanka*. Colombo: Social Scientists' Association, 1998.

Jazeel, Tariq. "Literary Landscapes: Geography, Spatial Politics and Productions of the National in Michael Ondaatje's *Anil's Ghost*." (Unpublished paper delivered at ICES, Colombo, March 3, 2005).

Jewinski, Ed. *Michael Ondaatje: Express Yourself Beautifully*. Toronto: ECW Press, 1994.

Johnson Richard *et al.*, eds. *Making Histories: Studies in History Writing and Politics*. London: Hutchinson & Co, 1982.

Johnston, John. 1992. "Translation as Simulacrum." In *Rethinking Translation: Discourse, Subjectivity, Ideology*, ed. Venuti, 42-56. London: Routledge 1992.

Kandiah, Thiru. "Disinherited Englishes: The Case of Lankan English." *Navasilu* 4 (1981): 92-110.

———. "Inadequate Responses and the Attenuation of Creativity: Sri Lankan English Fiction of the Insurgency of 1971." In *The Writer as Historical Witness: Studies in Commonwealth Literature*, ed. Thumboo and Kandiah, 393-408. Singapore: Unipress, 1995.

———. "New Varieties of English: The Creation of the Paradigm and its Radicalization." *Navasilu* 10 (1990): 126-135.

———. "Towards a Lankan Canon in English Creative Writing: Subversions of Post-colonialism and the Resisting Representations of Chitra Fernando's Fictional Voice." *Phoenix* VI & VII (1997): 47-54.

Larsen, Svend Erik. "Landscape, Identity and War." *New Literary History* 35, no. 3 (2004): 469-490.

Lefevere, André, ed. *Translation History Culture*. London and New York: Routledge, 1992.

Lewis, Frederick. *Sixty-four Years in Ceylon: Reminiscences of Life and Adventure*. Colombo: The Colombo Apothecaries Company, 1926.

Lewis, Philip E. "The Measure of Translation Effects." In *Difference in Translation,* ed. Graham, 31-62. Ithaca: Cornell U.P, 1985.

Ludowyk, Evelyn F. C. *The Modern History of Ceylon*. London: Weidenfeld & Nicolson, 1966.

MacIntyre, Ernest. "Outside of Time: *Running in the Family*." In *Spider Blues: Essays on Michael Ondaatje*, ed. Solecki, 315-319. Montréal: Véhicule Press, 1985.

Marshall, Henry. *Ceylon: A General Description of the Island and Its Inhabitants*. London: William H. Allen and Co., 1846. Reprint, Dehiwala: Tisara Prakasakayo, 1982.

Matthews, S. Leigh. "'The Bright Bone of a Dream": Drama, Performativity, Ritual, and Community in Michael Ondaatje's *Running in the Family*." *Biography* 23, no.2 (2000): 352-371.

Maundeville, Sir John. *The voiage and travaile of Sir John Maundeville, Kt.* Edited by James Orchard Halliwell-Phillipps, 1839. Reprint, London: F.S. Ellis, 1866.

Mehrez, Samia. 1992. "Translation and the Postcolonial Experience: The Francophone North African Text." In *Rethinking Translation: Discourse, Subjectivity, Ideology*, ed. Venuti, 120-138. London: Routledge 1992.

Mendis, Dushyanthi. "Finding One's Voice: Carl Muller's *The Jam Fruit Tree* and *Yakada Yaka*." *Navasilu* 15-16 (1998): 64-69.

Moore-Gilbert, Bart. *Postcolonial Theory: Context, Practices, Politics*. London: Verso, 1997.

Muller, Carl. *All God's Children*. Colombo: Vijitha Yapa, 2004.

___. *Children of the Lion.* New Delhi: Viking Penguin Books India, 1997.

___. *Colombo: A Novel.* New Delhi: Penguin Books India, 1995b.

___. *A Funny Thing Happened on the Way to the Cemetery.* New Delhi: Penguin Books India, 1995c.

___. "Historical Fiction: The Historical Sensibility of the Story-teller." *The Island.*

___. *The Jam Fruit Tree.* New Delhi: Penguin Books India, 1993.

___. *Once Upon a Tender Time.* New Delhi: Penguin Books India, 1995a.

___. *The Python of Pura Malai and Other Stories.* New Delhi: Penguin Books India, 1995d.

___. "'Righting' the Nation." *The Island.*

___. *Spit and Polish.* New Delhi: Penguin Books India, 1998.

___. *Yakada Yakā.* New Delhi: Penguin Books India, 1994.

Mundwiler, Leslie. *Michael Ondaatje: Word, Image, Imagination.* Vancouver: Talon Books, 1984.

Nergaard, Siri, ed., trans. *La teoria della traduzione nella storia.* Milano: Bompiani, 2002.

___. *Teorie contemporanee della traduzione.* Milano: Bompiani, 1995.

The New Shorter Oxford English Dictionary on Historical Principles. Oxford: Clarendon Press, 1993.

Ngugi wa Thiong'o. *Decolonising the Mind: The Politics of Language in African Literature.* Nairobi: East African Educational Publishers, 1986.

Niranjana, Tejaswini. *Siting Translation: History, Post-structuralism, and the Colonial Context.* Berkeley and Los Angeles: University of California Press, 1992.

Obeysekere, Ranjini. *The Sri Lankan Theatre in the Past Two Decades.* Colombo: Marga Institute, 2001.

Ondaatje, Michael. *Anil's Ghost.* London: Picador, 2000.

___. *The English Patient.* London: Picador, 1992.

___. *In the Skin of a Lion.* Toronto: McClelland and Stewart, 1987.
___. *Running in the Family.* London: Picador, 1982.
Parry, Benita. "Problems in Current Theories of Colonial Discourse." *Oxford Literary Review* 9, nos. 1&2 (1987): 27-58.
Pasco, Allan H. "Literature as Historical Archive." *New Literary History* 35, no. 3 (2004): 373-394.
Pepper, David, and Alan Jenkins. *The Geography of Peace and War.* London: Blackwell, 1985.
Perera, Sasanka. *Living with Torturers and Other Essays of Intervention: Sri Lankan Society, Culture and Politics in Perspective.* Colombo: ICES, 1999.
Perera, Suvendrini. "'We can be killed but we can never be silenced': Narratives of Coexistence in Recent Sri Lankan Fiction." *CRNLE Journal* (2000): 13-23. http://ehlt.flinders.edu.au/english/CRNLE/CRNLEjournal.html.
Perera, Walter. "Sri Lanka." *The Journal of Commonwealth Literature* 40 (2005): 235-251.
___. "Sri Lanka." *The Journal of Commonwealth Literature* 41 (2006): 215-229.
___. "Sri Lanka 2002." *The Journal of Commonwealth Literature* 39 (2004): 165-177.
___. "Sri Lanka 2003." *The Journal of Commonwealth Literature* 39 (2004): 178-188.
Perera-Rajasingham, Nimanthi, ed. *July '83 and After.* Nethra Special Issue. Colombo: ICES, 2003.
Petrilli, Susan, ed. *La traduzione.* Roma: Meltemi, 2000.
Popular Memory Group. 1982 "Popular Memory: Theory, Politics, Method." In *Making Histories: Studies in History Writing and Politics*, ed. Johnson *et al.*, 205-252. London: Hutchinson & Co, 1982.
Prasad, G. J. V. "Writing Translation. The Strange Case of the Indian English Novel." In *Postcolonial Translation: Theory and*

Practice, ed. Bassnett and Trivedi, 41-57. London: Routledge, 1999.
Pratt, Mary Louise. *Imperial Eyes: Travel Writing and Transculturation*. London: Routledge, 1992.
Punter, David. *Postcolonial Imaginings: Fictions of a New World Order*. Edinburgh: Edinburgh U.P., 2000.
Rabasa, José. "Allegories of *Atlas*." In *The Post-colonial Studies Reader*, ed. Ashcroft, Griffiths and Tiffin, 358-364. London: Routledge. 1995.
Rajasingham-Senanayake, Darini. "Identity on the Borderline: Modernity, New Ethnicities, and the Unmaking of Multiculturalism in Sri Lanka." In *The Hybrid Island*, ed. Silva, 41-60. Reprint, Colombo: The Social Scientists' Association, 2004a.
Ranasinghe, Anne. *Against Eternity and Darkness*. 1998. Reprint, Colombo: The English Writers' Cooperative of Sri Lanka, 2000
___. *At What Dark Point*. 1991. Reprint, Colombo: The English Writers' Cooperative of Sri Lanka, 1996.
___. *Desire and Other Stories*. 1994. Reprint, London: Minerva Press, 1999.
___. *A Long Hot Day*. Colombo: The English Writers' Cooperative of Sri Lanka, 2005.
___. *Not Even Shadows*. Colombo: The English Writers' Cooperative of Sri Lanka, 1991.
Reif-Hülser, Monika, ed. *Borderlands: Negotiating Boundaries in Post-colonial Writing*. ASNEL Papers 4. Amsterdam: Rodopi, 1999.
Riemenschneider, Dieter, ed. *The History and Historiography of Commonwealth Literature*. Tübingen: Gunter Narr Verlag, 1983.
Robinson, Douglas. *Translation and Empire: Postcolonial Theories Explained*. Manchester: St. Jerome Publishing, 1997.
___. *The Translator's Turn*. Baltimore: The John Hopkins U.P., 1991.

Rushdie, Salman. *Imaginary Homelands: Essays and Criticism 1981-1991*. London: Granta Books, 1991.
___. *Midnight Children*. London: Vintage, 1995.
___. *The Moor's Last Sigh*. London: Vintage, 1996.
Ryan, Simon. *The Cartographic Eye: How Explorers Saw Australia* Cambridge: Cambridge U. P., 1996.
Said, Edward. *Culture and Imperialism*. London: Chatto & Windus, 1993.
___. *Orientalism*. 1978. Reprint, London: Penguin, 2003.
___. *The World, the Text, and the Critic*. Cambridge, Mass.: Harvard U.P., 1983.
Saklofske, Jon. "The Motif of the Collector and Implications of Historical Appropriation in Ondaatje's Novels." *CLCWeb: Comparative Literature and Culture* 6, no. 3 (2004): http://docs.lib.purdue.edu/clcweb/vol6/iss3/7.
Samarakkody, Minoli. "'Orientalism' in the Writings of Leonard Woolf and in the Critical Response to Them." *Phoenix: Sri Lankan Journal of English in the Commonwealth* 5, nos. V & VI (1997): 73-83.
Sanghera, Sandeep. "Touching the Language of Citizenship in Ondaatje's *Anil's Ghost*." *CLCWeb: Comparative Literature and Culture* 6, no.3 (2004): http://docs.lib.purdue.edu/clcweb/vol6/iss3/8.
Sarvan, Charles P. "Carl Muller's Trilogy and the Burghers of Sri Lanka." *World Literature Today* 71, no. 3 (1997): 527-532.
___. "The Writer as Historical Witness: With Reference to the Novels of Peter Nazareth." In *The Writer as Historical Witness: Studies in Commonwealth Literature*, ed. Thumboo and Kandiah, 64-72. Singapore: Unipress, 1995.
Scanlan, Margaret. "*Anil's Ghost* and Terrorism Time." *Studies in the Novel* 36, no. 3 (2004): 302-317.
Schiffrin, Deborah, Deborah Tannen, and Heidi Hamilton, eds. *The Handbook of Discourse Analysis*. Oxford: Blackwell, 2003.

Schleiermacher, Friedrich, trans. "On the Different Methods of Translating.' In *The Translation Studies Reader*, ed. Venuti, 43-63. Abingdon, Oxon and New York: Routledge, 2004.

Schwarz, Henry, and Sangeeta Ray, eds. *A Companion to Postcolonial Studies*. Oxford: Blackwell, 2000.

Selden, Raman. *A Reader's Guide to Contemporary Literary Theory*. Brighton: The Harvester Press, 1985.

Selvadurai, Shyam. *Funny Boy*. New Delhi: Penguin Books India, 1994.

Silva, Neluka. "Debunking Ethnic Labels." *Frontline* 16, no. 4 (1999): http://www.hinduonnet.com/fline/fl1604/16040750.htm.

___. ed. *The Gendered Nation: Contemporary Writings from South Asia*. New Delhi: Sage Publications, 2004b.

___. ed. *The Hybrid Island*. 2002. Reprint, Colombo: The Social Scientists' Association, 2004a.

___. "Situating the Hybrid 'Other' in an Era of Conflict: Representations of the Burgher in Contemporary Writings in English." In *The Hybrid Island*, ed. Silva, 104-126. Colombo: The Social Scientists' Association, 2004a.

Silva, Neluka, and Rajiva Wijesinha, eds. *Across Cultures: Issues of Identity in Contemporary British and Sri Lankan Writing*. Colombo: The British Council, 2001.

Simon, Sherry. "The Language of Cultural Difference: Figures of Alterity in Canadian Translation." In *Rethinking Translation: Discourse, Subjectivity, Ideology*, ed. Venuti, 159-176. London: Routledge 1992.

___. "Translating and Interlingual Creation in the Contact Zone. Border Writing in Quebec." In *Postcolonial Translation: Theory and Practice*, ed. Bassnett and Trivedi, 58-74. London: Routledge, 1999.

Slemon, Stephen. "Monuments of Empire: Allegory/Counter-Discourse/Post-colonial Writing." *Kunapipi* 9, no. 3 (1987): 1-16.

Smith, Neil, and Anne Godlewska. *Geography and Empire*. Oxford: Blackwell, 1994.

Solecki, Sam, ed. *Spider Blues: Essays on Michael Ondaatje*. Montréal: Véhicule Press, 1985.

Spivak, Gayatri Chakravorty. *A Critique of Postcolonial Reason: Towards A History of the Vanishing Present*. Cambridge: Harvard U.P., 1999.

___. *In Other Worlds: Essays in Cultural Politics*. New York: Methuen, 1988.

___. "The Politics of Translation." In *Destabilizing Theory: Contemporary Feminist Debates*, ed. Michèle Barret and Anne Phllips, 177-200. Cambridge: Polity Press, 1993.

Spurr, David. *The Rhetoric of Empire*. Durham and London: Duke U.P., 1993.

Steiner, George. *After Babel*. Oxford and New York: Oxford U.P., 1975.

Sumathy. *Thin Veils, In the Shadow of the Gun & The Wicked Witch (Performing Act/ivism)*. Colombo: ICES, 2003.

Thumboo, Edwin, and Thiru Kandiah, eds. *The Writer as Historical Witness: Studies in Commonwealth Literature*. Singapore: Unipress, 1995.

Tiffin, Chris, and Alan Lawson, eds. *De-Scribing Empire: Postcolonialism and Textuality*. London and New York: Routledge, 1994.

Tiffin, Helen. "Post-colonial Literatures and Counter-Discourse." *Kunapipi* 9, no. 3 (1987): 17-38.

Tompkins, Jane. "Textuality, Morality and the Problem of History." In *"Race", Writing, and Difference*, ed Gates, 59-67. Chicago: University of Chicago Press, 1985.

Totosy de Zepetnek, Steve. "Michael Ondaatje's *The English Patient*, 'History,' and the Other." *CLCWeb: Comparative Literature and Culture* 1, no. 4, (1999): http://docs.lib.purdue.edu/clcweb/vol1/iss4/8.

Turci, Monica. "People In-Between: *Running in the Family* as Fictional Biography." In *Borderlands: Negotiating Boundaries in Post-colonial Writing*, ASNEL Papers 4, ed. Reif-Hülser, 247-254. Amsterdam: Rodopi, 1999.

Tymoczko, Maria. "Post-colonial Writing and Literary Translation." In *Postcolonial Translation: Theory and Practice*, ed. Bassnett and Trivedi, 19-40. London: Routledge, 1999.

___. "Translation and Political Engagement. Activism, Social Change and the Role of Translation in Geopolitical Shifts." *Translator* 6, no. 1 (2000): 23-47.

University Teachers for Human Rights. www.uthr.org.lk.

Uwajeh, M. K. C. "The Task of the Translator Revisited in Performative Translatology." *Babel* 47, no. 3 (2001): 228-247.

Venuti, Lawrence, ed. "Introduction." *Translator* 4, no. 2 (1998): 135-144.

___. *Rethinking Translation: Discourse, Subjectivity, Ideology.* London: Routledge, 1992.

___. *The Translator's Invisibility: A History of Translation.* 1995. Reprint, Abingdon: Oxon and New York: Routledge, 2002.

___. ed. *The Translation Studies Reader*, 2nd ed. Abingdon, Oxon and New York: Routledge, 2004.

Walker, Vasuki. "The Image of the Burghers in Carl Muller's Trilogy: Fact, Fiction or Faction?" *Navasilu* 15-16 (1998): 90-103.

White, Hayden. *Tropics of Discourse: Essays in Cultural Criticism.* 1978. Reprint, Baltimore: The John Hopkins U.P, 1990.

Wickramasinghe, Nira. "From Hybridity to Authenticity: the Biography of a Few Kandyan Things." In *The Hybrid Island*, ed. Silva, 71-92. Colombo: The Social Scientists' Association, 2004a.

Wickramasinghe, Wimal. *Sinenglish: A De-hegemonized Variety of English in Sri Lanka.* Nugegoda: 2000.

___. *Sri Lanka in the Modern Age: A History of Contested Identities.* London: C. Hurst & Co., 2006.

Wijenaike, Punyakante. *Amulet.* Sri Lanka: n.p., 1994.

Wijesinha, Rajiva. *Acts of Faith*. New Delhi: Navrang, 1985.
___. "Editorial" *Journal of Commonwealth Literature* 33, no. 1 (1998): 1-3.
___. *Servants. A Cycle*. Colombo: McCallum Books, 1995.
___. "Spices and Sandcastles: The Exotic Historians of Sri Lanka." In *Across Cultures: Issues of Identity in Contemporary British and Sri Lankan Writing*, ed. Silva and Wijesinha, 11-20. Colombo: The British Council, 2001.
Woolf, Leonard. *Diaries in Ceylon 1908-1911: Records of a Colonial Administrator & Stories from the East*. Reprint, London: Hogarth Press, 1962.
___. *The Village in the Jungle*. 1913. Reprint, London: Chatto & Windus, 1951
Young, Robert J. C. *Colonial Desire: Hybridity in Theory, Culture and Race*. London: Routledge, 1995.
Zabus, Chantal. "Relexification." In *The Post-colonial Studies Reader*, ed. Ashcroft, Griffiths and Tiffin, 314-318. London: Routledge.1995.
Zaccaria, Paola. *Mappe senza frontiere: Cartografie letterarie dal Modernismo al Transnazionalismo*. Bari: Palomar, 1999.
Zoppi, Isabella Maria, ed. *Routes of the Roots: Geography and Literature in the English-Speaking Countries*. Roma: Bulzoni, 1998.

STUDIES IN ENGLISH LITERATURES

Edited by Koray Melikoğlu

ISSN 1614-4651

1   *Özden Sözalan*
      The Staged Encounter
      Contemporary Feminism and Women's Drama
      2nd, revised editon
      ISBN 3-89821-367-6

2   *Paul Fox (ed.)*
      Decadences
      Morality and Aesthetics in British Literature
      ISBN 3-89821-573-3

3   *Daniel M. Shea*
      James Joyce and the Mythology of Modernism
      ISBN 3-89821-574-1

4   *Paul Fox and Koray Melikoğlu (eds.)*
      Formal Investigations
      Aesthetic Style in Late-Victorian and Edwardian Detective Fiction
      ISBN 978-3-89821-593-0

5   *David Ellis*
      Writing Home
      Black Writing in Britain Since the War
      ISBN 978-3-89821-591-6

6   *Wei H. Kao*
      The Formation of an Irish Literary Canon in the Mid-Twentieth Century
      ISBN 978-3-89821-545-9

7   *Bianca Del Villano*
      Ghostly Alterities
      Spectrality and Contemporary Literatures in English
      2nd, revised editon
      ISBN 978-3-89821-714-9

8   *Melanie Ann Hanson*
      Decapitation and Disgorgement
      The Female Body's Text in Early Modern English Drama and Poetry
      ISBN 978-3-89821-605-5

9   *Shafquat Towheed (ed.)*
      New Readings in the Literature of British India, c.1780-1947
      ISBN 978-3-89821-673-9

10   *Paola Baseotto*
      "Disdeining life, desiring leaue to die"
      Spenser and the Psychology of Despair
      ISBN 978-3-89821-567-1

11   *Annie Gagiano*
     Dealing with Evils
     Essays on Writing from Africa
     ISBN 978-3-89821-867-2

12   *Thomas F. Halloran*
     James Joyce: Developing Irish Identity
     A Study of the Development of Postcolonial Irish Identity in the Novels of James Joyce
     ISBN 978-3-89821-571-8

13   *Pablo Armellino*
     Ob-scene Spaces in Australian Narrative
     An Account of the Socio-topographic Construction of Space in Australian Literature
     ISBN 978-3-89821-873-3

14   *Lance Weldy*
     Seeking a Felicitous Space on the Frontier
     The Progression of the Modern American Woman in O. E. Rölvaag, Laura Ingalls Wilder, and Willa Cather
     ISBN 978-3-89821-535-0

15   *Rana Tekcan*
     The Biographer and the Subject
     A Study on Biographical Distance
     ISBN 978-3-89821-995-2

16   *Paola Brusasco*
     Writing Within/Without/About Sri Lanka
     Discourses of Cartography, History and Translation in Selected Works by Michael Ondaatje and Carl Muller
     ISBN 978-3-8382-0075-0

FORTHCOMING (MANUSCRIPT WORKING TITLES)

Kevin Cole
Levity's Rainbow
Menippean Poetics in Swift, Fielding, and Sterne
ISBN 3-89821-654-3

Zeynep Z. Atayurt
'Excessive' Embodiment in Contemporary Women's Writing
ISBN 978-3-89821-978-5

Fatma Tuba Terci
Postmodern Goddesses in Contemporary Chicana Feminist Novel
Peel my Love Like an Onion, Caramelo, or, Puro Cuento: A Novel and Face of an Angel
ISBN 978-3-8382-0023-1

Geetha Ganga
Historicizing Somalia through Literary Narrative
The Fiction of Nuruddin Farah
ISBN 978-3-8382-0083-5

Series Subscription

Please enter my subscription to the series **Studies in English Literatures**, ISSN 1614-4651, as follows:

- ☐ complete series   OR   ☐ English-language titles
                                                                  ☐ German-language titles

starting with
- ☐ volume # 1
- ☐ volume # ___
  - ☐ please also include the following volumes: #___, ___, ___, ___, ___, ___, ___
- ☐ the next volume being published
  - ☐ please also include the following volumes: #___, ___, ___, ___, ___, ___, ___

- ☐ 1 copy per volume   OR   ☐ ___ copies per volume

Subscription within Germany:

You will receive every title on 1st publication at the regular bookseller's price incl. s & h and VAT.

Payment:
☐ Please bill me for every volume.
☐ Lastschriftverfahren: Ich/wir ermächtige(n) Sie hiermit widerruflich, den Rechnungsbetrag je Band von meinem/unserem folgendem Konto einzuziehen.

Kontoinhaber: _____ Kreditinstitut: _____
Kontonummer: _____ Bankleitzahl: _____

International Subscription:

Payment (incl. s & h and VAT) in advance for
- ☐ 10 volumes/copies (€ 319.80)   ☐ 20 volumes/copies (€ 599.80)
- ☐ 40 volumes/copies (€ 1,099.80)

Please send my books to:

NAME _____ DEPARTMENT _____
ADDRESS _____
POST/ZIP CODE _____ COUNTRY _____
TELEPHONE _____ EMAIL _____

date/signature _____

Please fax to: **0511 / 262 2201 (+49 511 262 2201)**
or mail to: *ibidem*-Verlag, Julius-Leber-Weg 11, D-30457 Hannover, Germany
or send an e-mail: ibidem@ibidem-verlag.de

***ibidem*-**Verlag

Melchiorstr. 15

D-70439 Stuttgart

info@ibidem-verlag.de

www.ibidem-verlag.de
www.ibidem.eu
www.edition-noema.de
www.autorenbetreuung.de

Zeitfracht Medien GmbH
Ferdinand-Jühlke-Straße 7,
99095 - DE, Erfurt
produktsicherheit@zeitfracht.de